KOREAN BARBECUE AT HOME

KOREAN BARBECUE AT HOME

50 TRADITIONAL RECIPES
TO ENTERTAIN FAMILY AND FRIENDS

SARA UPSHAW

Photography by Antonis Achilleos

ROCKRIDGE
PRESS

For general information on our other products and services or to obtain technical support, please contact our Customer Care Department within the United States at (866) 744-2665, or outside the United States at (510) 253-0500.

Rockridge Press publishes its books in a variety of electronic and print formats. Some content that appears in print may not be available in electronic books, and vice versa.

TRADEMARKS: Rockridge Press and the Rockridge Press logo are trademarks or registered trademarks of Callisto Media Inc. and/or its affiliates, in the United States and other countries, and may not be used without written permission. All other trademarks are the property of their respective owners. Rockridge Press is not associated with any product or vendor mentioned in this book.

Interior and Cover Designer: Stephanie Sumulong
Art Producer: Janice Ackerman
Editor: Cecily McAndrews
Production Editor: Matthew Burnett
Production Manager: Martin Worthington

Photography: ©2021 Antonis Achilleos. Food styling by Rishon Hanners.

Author photograph courtesy of Todd Lind.

Paperback ISBN: 978-1-63807-901-9
eBook ISBN: 978-1-63807-702-2
R0

For my halmoni,
who always made sure I had banchan.

사랑해요

BAECHU GEOTJEORI, FRESH KIMCHI; PAGE 44

CONTENTS

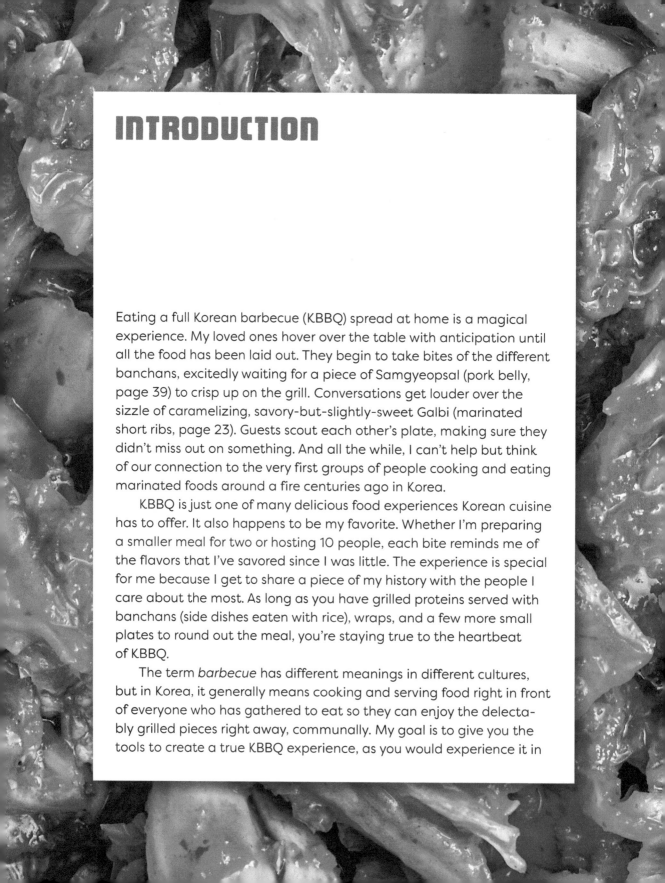

INTRODUCTION

Eating a full Korean barbecue (KBBQ) spread at home is a magical experience. My loved ones hover over the table with anticipation until all the food has been laid out. They begin to take bites of the different banchans, excitedly waiting for a piece of Samgyeopsal (pork belly, page 39) to crisp up on the grill. Conversations get louder over the sizzle of caramelizing, savory-but-slightly-sweet Galbi (marinated short ribs, page 23). Guests scout each other's plate, making sure they didn't miss out on something. And all the while, I can't help but think of our connection to the very first groups of people cooking and eating marinated foods around a fire centuries ago in Korea.

KBBQ is just one of many delicious food experiences Korean cuisine has to offer. It also happens to be my favorite. Whether I'm preparing a smaller meal for two or hosting 10 people, each bite reminds me of the flavors that I've savored since I was little. The experience is special for me because I get to share a piece of my history with the people I care about the most. As long as you have grilled proteins served with banchans (side dishes eaten with rice), wraps, and a few more small plates to round out the meal, you're staying true to the heartbeat of KBBQ.

The term *barbecue* has different meanings in different cultures, but in Korea, it generally means cooking and serving food right in front of everyone who has gathered to eat so they can enjoy the delectably grilled pieces right away, communally. My goal is to give you the tools to create a true KBBQ experience, as you would experience it in a true KBBQ restaurant; however, some concessions must be made for heat sources and dietary restrictions. Today, the heat sources in restaurants are different from those in households, so I'll show you different ways to find the one that works for you. Most think of gogi-gui (grilled meat) when picturing a full KBBQ spread, but I've included a few plant-based options, like Oyster Mushroom Bulgogi (page 35) and Gochujang Eggplant Gui (page 34), while using traditional foundations, so more people can enjoy this cuisine I love so dearly. Because of Buddhist influences (and practicality; meat was expensive) there are so many vegetarian dishes in Korean cuisine. They pair very nicely with your main grilled dishes, whether you're eating meat or not.

This cookbook is not meant to give you strict rules on how to make KBBQ at home. Instead, think of it as a guide to encourage you and give you confidence in the basics, which you can tailor to your needs and preferences. There isn't a wrong way to savor KBBQ. After all, the reason I know how to cook is because of the thousands of hours of research and decades of practice honing my skills in the kitchen. Any chance I had to feed someone, I took it. So basically, practice and passion make progress toward perfection. There are so many methods of creating the perfect bundles of different flavors and textures and delightfully stuffing them into your mouth. That's the beauty of KBBQ: No one walks away unsatisfied, because there is something for everyone.

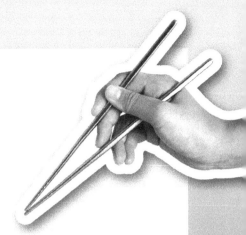

CHAPTER ONE

KOREAN BARBECUE 101

This chapter will set you up to begin making Korean barbecue on your own. We'll cover a bit of history and the joys of making it so that you know why this cuisine is so important to folks like me. Then, we'll go into the components of the meal, cooking sources, and what you will need in your pantry and kitchen to create and host barbecue for your family and friends.

A BRIEF HISTORY

Before there were floods of AYCE (all-you-can-eat) KBBQ, there was the simple need to preserve food in Korea. Specifically, the Goguryeo people, from 37 BCE to 668 CE, marinated meat for preservation. Maekjeok (doenjang marinated pork, page 28) is pork seasoned with doenjang, a fermented soybean paste, then cooked on skewers over the fire. This dish went through many iterations—it was once only served to royalty—eventually evolving into Bulgogi (thinly sliced marinated beef, page 22), one of the most popular Korean dishes. The demand for bulgogi pushed the rise of beef consumption, making it more available for grilling. The popularity of KBBQ restaurants grew after meat became less expensive and could be served in larger quantities on any occasion.

When Koreans started to immigrate to the United States, they brought with them the food preparation methods that reminded them of home. Consequently, in the early 1900s, the United States saw a proliferation of Koreatowns (Los Angeles is one of the most well-known). In the 1970s, people would travel to these Koreatowns in order to eat KBBQ. But today, KBBQ restaurants have become more common, and although its rise in mainstream popularity in the United States has been slow, Korean cuisine is definitely making its mark with those who love its bold flavors.

THE JOY OF KOREAN BARBECUE

Each culture has its own way of enjoying a large dinner for special occasions. Large-format meals—like hot pot and raclette, which are both cousins to KBBQ—are communal events that are meant to be eaten while cooking. In essence, large dinners are about the experience. When you're watching a raw piece of food transform into something so mouthwatering, anticipating it being done to perfection, and enjoying the wait with your loved ones, there's something really special about when you actually get to eat it. The joy that lies at the heart of these dinners is built in real time, right in front of you, with the people you care about while enjoying a shared experience with one communal goal: eating a delicious meal.

And I can't talk about the KBBQ experience without mentioning the atmosphere of excitement and anticipation the cuisine creates. It can get a little loud when you are trying to get someone to pass the Baechu Kimchi (napa cabbage kimchi, page 42) or score a piece of Dwaeji Bulgogi (spicy marinated pork, page 27). Far from a sedentary experience, KBBQ stirs a lot of movement and interaction between people and tables. There's no way your time at the table will be boring.

But that's not all. KBBQ is so popular not just because of the experience but because of the sheer variety it offers. The options are never-ending. In one sitting, you can eat the hottest and spiciest of foods, and switch over to refreshing and cooling accompaniments. Your mouth will experience textures ranging from crunchy lettuce in a ssam bundle to soft rice for the banchans, as well as chewy noodles. And the flavors . . . *Ahhh*, the flavors. The various flavors in KBBQ range from the sharp spiciness of gochugaru (Korean red pepper flakes) to the deep umami notes from ingredients like soy sauce and doenjang. A touch of sweetness is always present, but never outshines the other flavors.

THE COMPONENTS

Even if you've dined at a KBBQ restaurant before or had the pleasure of someone making this meal for you in their home, it can seem intimidating to make it yourself just because of the simple fact that there is a lot of dishware used to make and serve the meal. Although it is a good plan to have a dishwashing helper on hand, making the meal does not need to be overwhelming. You can prepare many of the components ahead of time. Plus, every time I've made this meal, it has been different, so there is a lot of flexibility to improvise. This section will break down the backbone of a KBBQ meal.

THE GRILL EVENT

What can go on the grill? Well, lots of things. The main proteins will rightfully take center stage at this event, with the marinades (which are all inter-changeable with the various proteins) playing supporting roles. Here is a list of some traditional and less traditional (but tradition-inspired) options.

Beef

When it comes to KBBQ, beef comes in many flavors and forms. You'll find as many marinated as unmarinated cuts of meat. While Galbi (marinated short ribs, page 23) and Bulgogi (thinly sliced marinated beef, page 22)—made from rib eye—are both very common, you'll find paper-thin slices of beef bris-ket, as well. The sides are meant to give balance, so an unmarinated piece of beef is meant to be eaten with flavor-rich dipping sauces and banchans.

Chicken

Chicken thighs, and dark meat generally, are best for KBBQ. They have so much more flavor and are very forgiving with heat, so they don't dry out. Typically, KBBQ chicken is marinated in either a spicy or savory sauce, both of which have a slight touch of sweetness.

Pork

Pork is one of the most popular proteins for KBBQ. The different cuts and tex-tures play well with all the various flavors. Pork shoulder can be marinated in either spicy or savory flavors, while pork belly is usually unseasoned to let the dipping sauces shine. Usually, you would start barbecuing with something like pork belly so the fat can render out and provide a nonstick surface for every-thing else.

Duck

Unless a KBBQ restaurant specializes in duck, you usually won't see this pro-tein on the menu. It's a bit of a luxury item, but the flavors and texture hold up well with Korean ingredients and marinades. This is a good choice if you're looking for something unique but still tasty.

Shrimp

Seafood wouldn't usually be served with the more common meats, like beef and pork, but it's not unheard of; there are restaurants that specialize in KBBQ seafood. Shrimp is a great choice if you're looking for variety because it marinates and cooks quickly, just like the thinly cut pieces of beef or pork. You can leave the shells on—and actually eat them, if they are grilled, for some extra crunch—or you can peel the shrimp beforehand.

Squid

Another seafood option that marinates well and has a great texture is squid. You can use both the body and the tentacles, presliced for the grill, or you can grill it whole to make it easier to handle and cut it after it comes off the grill.

Tofu

Any meatless protein will work with the marinades, but tofu is great because it provides a blank canvas. Make sure to use firm tofu so it doesn't break apart on the grill, drain it if it's packed in water, and use a delicious marinade to load it up with flavor.

Hearty Vegetables

In chapter 2, I suggest a few vegetables to sub in for the animal proteins (jackfruit, eggplant, and oyster mushrooms). As long as the vegetable can handle the marinade, it can be used for KBBQ.

VEGETABLES ON THE GRILL

Grilling vegetables alongside proteins is very much a part of KBBQ. They almost turn into banchans and fit perfectly inside a lettuce wrap with a protein. Trumpet mushrooms, white onion slices, and garlic slivers are the most common vegetables used in KBBQ. Any mushroom would be great, and shallots work well, too. Summer squash and sweet or spicy peppers are not traditional but would also go well on the grill. Whatever vegetables you choose, slice them thin to cook quickly, and don't marinate or season them. They are perfect bites for the dipping sauces.

One suggestion is putting kimchi on the grill, as well as serving it cold on the side. The sear brings out a level of deep flavor that almost tastes like a dry version of kimchi stew. Precut bite-size pieces are great. Don't be afraid to get some char on it and let the ends crisp up a bit.

DIPPING SAUCES

Dipping sauces help bring flavor and balance to each bite. Even though many people have their favorite protein and sauce combinations, you can use any of the sauces however you like.

Gireumjang 기름장 Salt and Sesame Oil Dipping Sauce

As simple as this dipping sauce is, it has so much flavor. Pour about 1 teaspoon of a coarse salt (like kosher salt) into a small bowl, then drizzle 1 tablespoon of toasted sesame oil on top. Coarse salt is preferable to table salt because it sticks to whatever unmarinated protein it touches and amplifies the protein's flavor instead of overpowering it. Make sure the sesame oil is toasted. Black pepper is a nice addition.

Ssamjang 쌈장 Fermented Soybean and Chili Dipping Sauce

Ssamjang (page 36) is one of the most popular dipping sauces for KBBQ. You can put a small dollop in your wrap or eat it with a fresh cucumber or carrot spear for a big punch of flavor. You can even purchase this sauce premade at any Korean grocery store, usually in a green container next to the doenjang (page 12) and gochujang (page 12), the two main ingredients in the sauce.

Saeujeot Jang 새우젓장 Spicy Fermented Shrimp Sauce

Saeujeot Jang (page 37) is usually served with bossam, pork belly that is boiled and wrapped in a cabbage leaf. Use this dipping sauce only with main proteins that are not marinated; otherwise, the flavors will be overwhelming. A Korean grocery store will be your best bet to find the main ingredient, saeujeot (salted fermented shrimp).

Green Onion and Vinegar Sauce

Green Onion and Vinegar Sauce (page 38) is not traditional, but I keep it on my own KBBQ table. The vinegar brightens any heavy foods that need a little lift. Feel free to drizzle some over your rice.

THE WRAPS (SSAM)

Most, not all, KBBQ will include wraps. KBBQ is generally eaten one bite at a time, each of which is served in an edible wrapper. The word *ssam* literally translates to wrap, so anything that can bundle the main protein with some sauce and banchans is considered a ssam. The three listed here are the most commonly served with KBBQ.

Sangchu 상추 Red Leaf Lettuce

Red leaf lettuce is the most common wrap. It's flexible enough to wrap every-thing into a bundle, but sturdy enough not to disintegrate when the leaf is fully loaded. Boston, Bibb, and butter lettuce also have the same amount of flexibility and structure. Use your hand to hold the sangchu while you're build-ing your ssam.

Kkaennip 깻잎 Perilla Leaves

Kkaennip is often mistaken for Japanese shiso leaves, but the two are very different in taste. Although both technically are types of perilla, the kkaennip has a stronger minty flavor, with a hint of licorice. It's wonderful wrapped around pork belly and is also great pickled or made into a kimchi. You can find kkaennip in Korean grocery stores either in a package of individual leaves or on their large stems.

Ssam Mu 쌈무 Marinated Radish Wraps

Mu is a Korean radish similar to Japanese daikon, but rounder, with a pale-green top on the root. To make Ssam Mu (page 50), slice the mu into paper-thin pieces, then marinate it in vinegar, salt, and sugar. Ssam mu makes a great wrap, and it can also be included in another ssam or eaten with a dollop of dipping sauce and protein.

THE SIDES (BANCHANS)

The main gogi-gui (grilled meat) might be the star of the show, but the banchans are just as beloved. These small side dishes ensure the meal isn't one note, which means you're more likely to keep eating. The balance of banchans with the main protein is the reason why KBBQ is so great for large groups. Everyone can find something that they'll love, and this usually becomes a topic of conversation. Anything can become a banchan, as long as it's served as a small portion. You can eat the side dishes with rice while you wait for items to grill or put some in wraps to give the ssam even more flavor. Chapter 3 offers a variety of banchan recipes that range from very simple, like Sigeumchi Namul (seasoned spinach, page 57) to very complex flavors, like Baechu Kimchi (napa cabbage kimchi, page 42). It's not unusual for many banchans to be served in one sitting. Usually, I make large batches and dish up smaller amounts for the actual meal.

OTHER GO-ALONGS

Yes, there's more. On top of the main protein, dipping sauces, wraps, and banchans, KBBQ often comes with small plates like Mandu (pork and kimchi dumplings, page 66), Korean Corn Cheese (page 68), and Haemul Pajeon (savory seafood pancakes, page 63). These are stand-alone dishes (not made to be eaten with rice or in ssams like banchans) that are served along with the meal.

Most small plate recipes, like Gyeran Mari (rolled egg omelet, page 65), are eaten throughout the meal, but a few are commonly eaten at the end, like Mul Naengmyeon (cold noodle soup, page 70) and Bokkeumbap (fried rice, page 74). You'll find these recipes in chapter 4.

BRINGING KOREAN BARBECUE HOME

Although it may seem intimidating, you absolutely can re-create the authentic KBBQ experience, where each diner cooks their own food, bite by bite, in your very own home. In this section, I'll cover manageable ways to create a full KBBQ both indoors and outdoors.

INDOOR GRILLS

The most common way friends and family enjoy KBBQ at home is indoors. There are a few options that work for heating sources. You can find extravagant grills made just for KBBQ, with high price points to match, but most indoor grills range from $40 to $80. The stovetop grill pan with a butane tabletop stove is the heating source that I use most. The high heat works wonders for caramelization. When I was growing up, we primarily used a flat electric griddle, which worked nicely because its large size made it easier to feed a large group.

Korean Barbecue Stovetop Grill Pan

The stovetop grill pan is the most popular way to cook KBBQ indoors at home. Since it's made to sit on top of a butane tabletop stove, you get even, high heat, which equals delicious caramelization. If you're not comfortable with this type of heat source, an electric griddle is another great option.

Korean Barbecue Electric Grill

Electric grills designed for KBBQ usually have grill grates, which provide a better chance for char; however, a lot of the delicious drippings will fall through into the pan underneath. For this reason, the pan is usually filled with water beforehand to prevent smoke.

Indoor Electric Griddle

These flat, nonstick, large-surface-area griddles are great to load up. They work well with vegetables, which soak up any of the marinade and drippings that come off of the main proteins; however, this does cause some of the meat to steam instead of char.

Raclette Grill

This type of grill is usually used for a Swiss dish that includes melted cheese, but it can also be used in a KBBQ setting. The electric heat sears the proteins on top of the grill while whatever you put in the small pans underneath gets broiled. This does entail a bit more cleanup, however.

OUTDOOR GRILLS

Grilling KBBQ outdoors is a wonderful treat. If you use charcoal, you can get even more layers of flavor, and you don't have to worry about your home potentially filling with smoke.

Tabletop Yakitori Charcoal Grill

If you have outdoor space, a tabletop Japanese yakitori-style grill works great. It actually mimics the restaurant charcoal grills the best. Try to find sut 숯 (wood) charcoal because it burns very cleanly and contains no added chemicals.

Tabletop Portable Propane Gas Grill

This type of grill is larger and more powerful than the butane tabletop grill (which is why it's for outdoor use only), but it will char just as nicely as the outdoor charcoal grill. Make sure to find one with a detachable lid so it doesn't take up too much space. This grill can be moved to the side of the table with the person designated to cook all of the main proteins.

WORKING WITH WHAT YOU HAVE

When it comes down to it, even if you don't have a tabletop grill and choose to have one person cook the proteins, there are still ways to enjoy KBBQ. One indoor method is to use the trusty stovetop, preferably with a cast-iron skillet so you can still get great caramelization. Cook quickly on high heat, but make sure not to crowd the pan to avoid steaming. And plan to have all the individual place settings, banchans, and small plates set out and ready to go so the last thing to fill the table is the cooked main protein.

You can also use a freestanding charcoal or propane grill outside. Leave your meat or vegetarian protein cut large so it's easier to handle and doesn't fall through the grill grates; you can cut it up smaller with kitchen scissors afterward. The cook time will still be quick, so use high heat to get that char without overcooking the protein. If you're grilling smaller marinated vegetables, thread them onto a skewer to grill, then transfer them to a serving platter.

KOREAN BARBECUE TOOLKIT

After you pick which grill and cooking method you want to use, you'll just need a few more items. After making a few KBBQ meals, you'll come up with your own set of must-have items.

COOKING UTENSILS

Everyone at the table can take finished items off the grill with their chopsticks, but you'll want at least a couple pairs of tongs dedicated to cooking on the grill: One should be used for raw items going on the grill, and the other for cooked items coming off the grill.

KITCHEN SCISSORS

Kitchen scissors are an essential tool for KBBQ (and Korean home cooking in general). They cut perfectly without having to get out a cutting board, and they are especially useful if you have large pieces on a freestanding grill that need to be made into bite-size pieces at the table.

INDIVIDUAL PLACE SETTINGS

You'll want one small plate, one set of chopsticks (metal if you'd like to make it traditionally Korean), one dinner spoon, and a small dipping bowl (for the sesame oil and salt) for each person at the table. A small bowl for rice is optional.

SMALL BOWLS FOR BANCHANS

Have a set of matching small bowls for banchans. This will help differentiate the banchans from the small plates. The size also helps fit everything on the table.

PLATES FOR SMALL SIDES AND WRAPS

Use small plates for, well, the small plates. These plates work well for dishes like Haemul Pajeon (savory seafood pancakes, page 63) and for holding the different types of wraps.

SEPARATE PLATTERS FOR VEGETABLES TO GRILL AND MARINATED PROTEINS

Use separate large platters to hold anything about to be grilled.

KOREAN BARBECUE INGREDIENT STAPLES

The following is a list of staples for your KBBQ meal. Every ingredient is versatile and can be used in many recipes. These will be easiest to find in a Korean grocery store, but many large Asian grocery stores (and large international sections in general grocery stores) will have these items, as well. If your local grocery store doesn't have a large international section, you can buy these ingredients online (see Resources on page 90).

Gochujang 고추장 Fermented Chili Paste

Gochujang has a bit of a smoky flavor with a smooth and thick consistency. The spiciness is not as sharp as sriracha, but it builds up as you keep eating it. You can find gochujang in different levels of spice, but it's usually at a medium heat. Keep in mind that this ingredient needs to be added to dishes the way tomato paste is, and that it isn't an all-purpose hot sauce. Because it is fermented and salted, if stored in the refrigerator, it should keep indefinitely.

Gochugaru 고춧가루 Korean Red Pepper Flakes

These flakes are from the same pepper that makes gochujang. The texture is coarse but consistent, with a smoky and a slightly fruity flavor. Just like gochujang, gochugaru is usually sold in a medium heat level. I highly recommend finding this specific type of chili flake because non-Korean varieties do not substitute well.

Doenjang 된장 Fermented Soybean Paste

Doenjang is a fermented paste made from soybeans. It has similarities to miso but is coarser in texture and usually deeper in umami flavor. Add heat or liquid to soften the paste even further. You can use doenjang anywhere you want to add a deeper flavor profile. Doenjang will not spoil if kept in the refrigerator, but the consistency might harden if it's not kept in an airtight container.

Ganjang 간장 Soy Sauce

Different countries have different types of soy sauce with different flavors. Korean soy sauce is mostly broken down into two categories: a lighter version that's a by-product of doenjang called guk-ganjang (soup soy sauce), and an all-purpose ganjang that is naturally brewed for fermentation. The soup soy sauce is used primarily in soups to bring a lighter flavor and lighter color to the broth. I suggest using Korean soup soy sauce as a vegan alternative to fish sauce. Both kinds of soy sauce can be found in my pantry, but I regularly grab the all-purpose soy sauce because I don't mind a darker color and always seek out deeper flavors.

Maesilcheong 매실청 Plum Syrup

This plum syrup is commonly used to sweeten dishes, and it is wonderful in marinades. It's made from fermenting tart green plums in sugar. The taste is lighter than just using granulated sugar and sweeter than just using fruit. You'll often hear people talk about wanting marinades and braises to be shiny in Korean cuisines, and this plum syrup is the ingredient that makes that happen. If you can't find maesilcheong, swap it out for honey. The taste will be slightly different, but a liquid sweetener is what you're looking for.

Chamgireum 참기름 Toasted Sesame Oil

The most important thing to know about sesame oil in Asian cuisine is that it should be purchased already toasted. Rather than using it to coat a pan or to fry something, this toasted oil adds extra flavor to dishes. Even when used in small amounts, it still makes a big impact. When shopping for toasted sesame oil, look for a darker color with a bit of a thick consistency (one that will coat the bottle instead of running down the sides).

Bokkeunkkae 볶은깨 Sesame Seeds

Sesame seeds are common in a variety of cultures. They can be used as a garnish, to add subtle flavors to a dish, or as the main ingredient in candies and pastries. Crush them to bring out even more of their flavor. Buy them roasted, or you can roast them in a dry pan on low heat.

Ssal 쌀 Short-Grain Rice

Korean meals use short-grain white rice because it gives a neutral flavor foundation and is sticky, which makes it easier to use chopsticks. Short-grain brown rice is another option, but even more popular is adding ingredients like black rice to short-grain white rice to make heukmi (literally translated, black rice). It turns the white grains purple and is more nutritious than plain white rice. Add 1 tablespoon of black rice for every 2 cups of white rice.

Aekjeot 액젓 Fish Sauce

Fish sauce is common across many Asian cultures, but there are many different types of Korean fish sauce made from different seafoods like anchovy or shrimp. This ingredient is made to give saltiness and umami at the same time. It deepens the flavor of soups like Kimchi Jjigae (kimchi stew, page 69) and banchans like Oi Muchim (spicy cucumber salad, page 47). For the purposes of these recipes, you can use any fish sauce.

Ssalsikcho 쌀식초 Rice Vinegar

Rice vinegar is not as sharp as distilled white vinegar; it has a mellower acidity that brightens any dish. It's a great ingredient to cut through any heavy flavors that need balance.

Saeujeot 새우젓 Salted Fermented Shrimp

Saeujeot is made with tiny shrimp that are salted and fermented. It has a sharp, high-pitched taste instead of the deep umami of much fermented seafood. Use saeujeot as you would use salt to season soups, sauces, and dishes.

KNIFE SKILLS

Knife skills are critical for KBBQ because cutting most of the protein very thin is crucial so that it can cook in just a few minutes.

KEEP IT THIN

The key to getting certain items to grill quickly is slicing everything as thin as possible. There are some cuts like Galbi (marinated short ribs, page 23) that will be thicker because of the bone, and I recommend that you don't cut plant-based proteins thinly because they will turn into mush. But generally, the goal is to slice the protein to about ⅛-inch thickness, if possible. In order to have a better handle on the meat, you can freeze it for about 30 minutes; this will harden it so that it's easier to cut. Consistency is essential, so whatever thickness you end up slicing, keep it all the same so that the pieces will all cook together in the same amount of time on the grill.

CUT ACROSS THE GRAIN

For beef and pork, you'll want to slice in a particular way to ensure each piece is tender. Cutting across the grain means to cut across the fiber lines instead of parallel to them. If you're not sure which way to go, slice two small pieces of your meat in different directions. If you've cut across the grain, you won't see lines that are running across the width of your piece.

HOW TO THINLY SLICE MEAT FOR BULGOGI

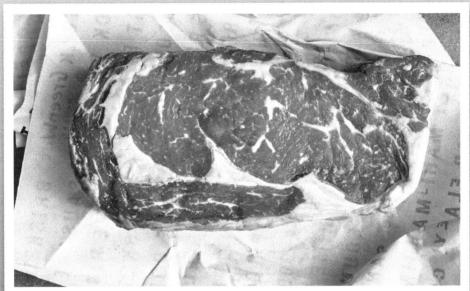

Freeze the rib eye steak for about **30** minutes to make it easier to handle.

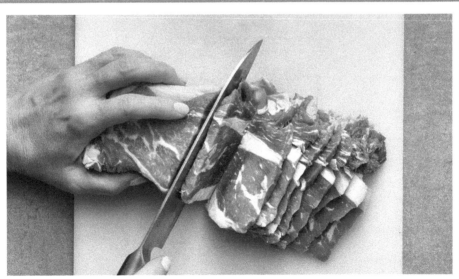

Slice across the grain of the meat into thin, even pieces, about ⅛ inch thick.

HOW TO MAKE A SSAM BUNDLE

Pick a ssam wrap. Use the palm of your hand to hold the leaf. For Ssam Mu (marinated radish wraps, page 50), build on a plate, or even in your hand—the traditional method. Put a main protein like Bulgogi (thinly sliced marinated beef, page 22) or Samgyeopsal (pork belly, page 39) on the wrap.

Layer on any dipping sauces and banchans of your choosing, like Ssam-jang (fermented soybean and chili dipping sauce, page 36) and Baechu Kimchi (napa cabbage kimchi, page 42).

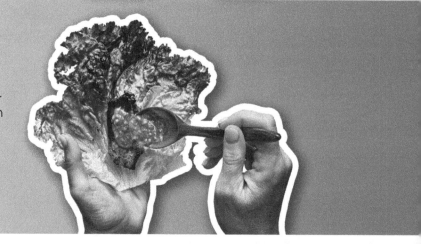

Wrap the ssam up and try to fit the whole bundle in your mouth. Stuffing your cheeks to the brim is very common!

HOW TO HOST A KOREAN BARBECUE FOR FAMILY OR GUESTS

Every time I've hosted a KBBQ at home, I've done it differently. There are too many wonderful combinations that can't be captured in one sitting, and sometimes you just need to do a little improvisation. Keep this in mind so you don't feel constrained.

PLANNING THE MENU

Before planning a menu, find out if your guests have any food allergies or aversions. It can be disheartening to skip this step only to find that your guests won't eat what you've made. To get started, estimate portion size. You can estimate about ½ pound (8 ounces) of meat or main protein per person. This can be a tough task, so I've provided a few menu choices for four, six, and eight people (see Korean Barbecue Menus on page 85). Each menu will have a variety of main proteins, banchans, and small plates.

Now, decide on the dishes. You'll want a balance of items that you can make ahead of time and some to make fresh. Think of the timing of the meal. If your main protein is Galbi (marinated short ribs, page 23), then that will take longer to cook, so you'll want to have a heavier small plate like Mandu (pork and kimchi dumplings, page 66), so that people aren't too hungry while they're waiting. The key to serving larger groups is to have a lot of banchans, even matching sets on both sides of the table, so the main protein is spread out. Definitely serve rice.

MAKE AHEAD

All of the marinated meats can be made ahead of time and stored either in the refrigerator for about two days or in the freezer for up to three months. The fermented banchans, like Baechu Kimchi (napa cabbage kimchi, page 42), require time to ferment, so you could make them a month ahead of time. I always try to have some type of stockpile in the refrigerator and freezer so I can throw together a KBBQ party quickly and just buy the few fresh ingredients. That way, on the day of, you won't be scrambling around trying to make everything at once.

WHO'S DOING THE COOKING

When KBBQ first started popping up stateside, there was a misconception that people wouldn't want to pay for a meal that they had to cook themselves. This proved to be untrue, obviously. Tabletop cooking is popular because it's fun. Nonetheless, there should be one or two dedicated people who are in charge of the grill; otherwise, the food will definitely burn. Usually, someone will plan to fill up first so they can take over cooking for whoever started at the beginning of the meal. If the grill is not on the table, the host (or a guest who loves to take charge) will cook the protein and bring it to the table when it's ready.

SECRETS TO SUCCESS

→ Use smaller individual plates to help everything fit on the table.

→ Make sure the room you're dining in is very well-ventilated.

→ At least one person will need to be in charge of flipping and watching the grilled items so that nothing burns. It's everyone's duty to make sure this point person also has a chance to eat.

→ To mimic the KBBQ restaurant experience, cook all of one protein before going to the next.

→ There's no need to try to fit every banchan and grilled piece into one bite. Instead try to eat many small combinations.

→ During the meal, if you're not using your chopsticks, lay them on your plate or bowl so the food ends don't touch the table.

→ Take your time enjoying this meal!

→ Before the meal starts, show your appreciation by reciting the traditional phrase, "Jal meokkesseumnida (jahl-muh-keh-ssum-ni-da)!" "(잘 먹겠습니다)!" which means, "I will eat well!"

PRESENTATION

The setup of the KBBQ table defies the logic of space, and yet somehow it all works. The table will, and should, be crowded. You will most likely bump into one another and need to move items around as the meal goes on. All of the main proteins, dipping sauces, wraps, banchans, and small plates should be served at the same time. If possible, the grill should be put in the middle so everyone can reach any food that is ready to go. Warn guests that everything close to the grill will be in the splatter zone (they'll want to move their drinks away).

WHAT TO DRINK WITH KOREAN BARBECUE

Koreans embrace a "work hard, play hard" mentality. While alcoholic beverages are usually not consumed at home in Korea, they do flow plentifully at restaurants with coworkers and friends, especially when food is involved. Soju and beer are the most common drinks that you'll find on a KBBQ table. They pair well with the meal and go down easily all through the evening. In chapter 5, you'll find a few beverages, like Subak Hwachae (watermelon punch, page 79), to sip on if you'd rather go the nonalcoholic route.

SOJU 소주 RICE WINE

Soju is, by far, the most popular liquor in Korea. This might be why most of the drinking games involve this libation. Unlike Japanese sake, which is fermented, soju is distilled and is on the sweeter side. The first round of soju is generally a shot, but people may sip the beverage as the meal continues. Somaek 소맥 is described as a cocktail, but really it's a popular drink with just a shot of soju—shot glass sometimes included—dunked in a large glass of beer. If you're pouring the soju into the beer, get a spoon and hit the middle of the beer glass to form bubbles that make the drink smooth. Hit hard enough, and you'll receive cheers.

MAEKJU 맥주 BEER

Beer is a very popular choice to accompany delicious bites hot off the grill. There are three top brands in Korea that you will find at KBBQ restaurants, but any extra-cold, light lager will pair well with the variety of flavors on the table. Be careful because in Korean drinking etiquette, your glass will be continuously filled for you.

PODOJU 포도주/와인 WINE

Wine isn't the most common drink offered when dining on gogi-gui, but it is quickly gaining popularity on the KBBQ table. With the range of flavors in the food, you can easily pair your favorite light- to medium-bodied reds and dry whites. Avoid heavy, full-bodied wines that will fill you up before the meal does. For spicy main courses, I recommend a chilled sauvignon blanc with only a hint of fruit and green peppery notes. With deeply savory main courses, a bright and earthy Sangiovese that has high acidity balances quite nicely.

BULGOGI, THINLY SLICED MARINATED BEEF; PAGE 22

PROTEINS AND DIPPING SAUCES

불고기 BULGOGI
THINLY SLICED MARINATED BEEF

Serves 4 / Prep time: 30 minutes, plus 30 minutes to freeze and 4 to 24 hours to marinate / **Cook time:** 6 minutes

As Korean cuisine has grown in popularity outside of Korea, bulgogi has emerged as the talisman of Korean dishes. Bulgogi can actually refer to any kind of meat that's marinated, but you'll find that it's most commonly prepared with beef. When you bite into a piece of bulgogi, you should taste salty umami with only a kiss of sweetness. You can also stir-fry it with onions and carrots to make it more substantial.

1 pound rib eye steak

½ cup soy sauce

2 tablespoons minced garlic

2 tablespoons toasted sesame oil

2 tablespoons plum syrup

2 teaspoons coarse ground black pepper

1. Freeze the steak for about 30 minutes to make it easier to handle. Once it is frozen, slice the steak across the grain into thin, even pieces, about ⅛ inch thick.

2. In a medium bowl, whisk together the soy sauce, garlic, oil, plum syrup, and pepper. Add the sliced beef and combine until the marinade is evenly incorporated. Cover and refrigerate the bowl and let the beef marinate for at least 4 hours, although 24 hours is best.

3. When you're ready to grill, shake off and discard any excess marinade from the beef. Grill the meat over medium-high heat for about 3 minutes per side, until you start to see caramelization. Don't overcrowd the bulgogi or the meat will steam instead of sear.

PAIRS WELL WITH: Try wrapping this bulgogi in red leaf lettuce with a dollop of Ssamjang (fermented soybean and chili dipping sauce, page 36), and some Baechu Kimchi (napa cabbage kimchi, page 42). If you're up for it, add a slice of raw garlic.

갈비 GALBI
MARINATED SHORT RIBS

Serves 4 / Prep time: 30 minutes, plus 4 to 24 hours to marinate /
Cook time: 10 minutes

Glistening and slightly charred galbi is one of the jewels of Korean barbecue. This recipe, referred to as "LA Galbi," uses flanken-style cut short ribs, meaning that they are cut across the bone. It's said that the "LA" part of the name comes from the fact that Korean immigrants to Los Angeles were the first to make this dish. But the "LA" could also represent the lateral cut across the bones. Either way, KBBQ lovers celebrate the invention of this savory creation.

3 pounds lateral-cut (flanken-style) bone-in short ribs

1 small yellow onion, coarsely chopped

1 large Asian pear, coarsely chopped

4 large garlic cloves

½ cup soy sauce

2 tablespoons plum syrup

2 tablespoons toasted sesame oil

1 tablespoon kosher salt

1 teaspoon coarse ground black pepper

1. Rinse the meat in cold water to clean off any bone fragments. Pat it dry with paper towels. Cut the meat into pieces with one bone each. Set aside in a large bowl.

2. In a food processor, blend the onion, pear, garlic, soy sauce, plum syrup, oil, salt, and pepper until the marinade is smooth and slightly foamed up from the fruit.

3. Pour the marinade into the bowl with the short ribs, and combine until evenly incorporated. Cover and refrigerate the bowl and let the short ribs marinate for at least 4 hours, although 24 hours is best.

4. When you're ready to grill, shake off and discard any excess marinade from the short ribs. Grill the meat over high heat for about 5 minutes per side, or until the pieces are brown and have charred bits.

PAIRS WELL WITH: Because you'll be biting off the bone, galbi works best with a spoonful of rice and a well-fermented banchan like Kkakdugi (radish kimchi, page 46).

등심 DEUNGSIM
MARINATED STRIP STEAK

Serves 4 / Prep time: 35 minutes, plus 4 to 24 hours to marinate /
Cook time: 10 minutes

If you find deungsim on the menu in a Korean barbecue restaurant, it usually won't be marinated. But, as luck would have it, you're making it at home, so you have the opportunity to give this tender, juicy steak even more flavor. The black pepper notes add a little more zing than you'll find in the bulgogi recipe. New York strip steaks are a great, tender choice, but any sirloin will do.

¼ **cup minced garlic**

3 **tablespoons packed dark brown sugar**

1 **tablespoon coarse ground black pepper**

½ **cup soy sauce**

¼ **cup toasted sesame oil**

2 **(1 pound, 1-inch-thick) New York strip steaks**

PAIRS WELL WITH: Sliced deungsim pairs well with any well-fermented banchan, like Baechu Kimchi (napa cabbage kimchi, page 42) or Kkakdugi (radish kimchi, page 46).

1. In a medium high-walled glass storage container, combine the garlic, brown sugar, pepper, soy sauce, and oil and stir. Add the steaks, flipping each steak to coat it with the marinade.

2. Cover and refrigerate the container and let the steaks marinate for at least 4 hours, although 24 hours is best. Flip the steaks halfway through marinating.

3. When you're ready to cook the steaks, set them on the counter for at least 30 minutes to bring them to room temperature. Shake off and discard any excess marinade from the steaks. Sear the steaks on the grill over medium-high heat for about 5 minutes per side to reach medium-rare (an internal temperature of 130°F). Transfer the steaks to a plate and let them rest for 5 minutes, then slice the meat against the grain into ½-inch pieces to serve.

MAKE-AHEAD TIP: Once the steaks are in the marinade, the deungsim can be stored in the freezer for up to three months. Thaw the meat in the refrigerator for one day before cooking.

닭불고기 DAK BULGOGI
MARINATED CHICKEN

Serves 4 / Prep time: 15 minutes, plus 4 to 24 hours to marinate / **Cook time:** 20 minutes

Dak bulgogi uses chicken instead of red meat. The flavor closely mimics teriyaki, but it doesn't have the sweetness that usually comes with the Japanese marinade and sauce. You can make it sweeter if you like, but make sure to keep the sweetness in the back seat so the soy sauce can drive.

8 boneless, skinless
  chicken thighs

¼ cup soy sauce

3 tablespoons toasted
  sesame oil

2 tablespoons
  minced garlic

1 tablespoon peeled
  grated fresh ginger

1 tablespoon rice vinegar

2 teaspoons coarse
  ground black pepper

1. Slice the chicken into thin, even pieces, about ½ inch thick, and remove any unwanted fat.

2. In a large bowl, whisk together the soy sauce, oil, garlic, ginger, vinegar, and pepper. Add the chicken pieces and combine until the marinade is evenly incorporated. Cover and refrigerate the bowl and let the chicken marinate for at least 4 hours, although 24 hours is best.

3. When you're ready to grill, shake off and discard any excess marinade from the chicken. Grill the pieces over medium-high heat for about 10 minutes per side, making sure not to move them around too much so that you can get some browning, until the juice runs clear and there is no pink in the center.

PAIRS WELL WITH: Dak bulgogi is perfect with a spoonful of rice and a spicy banchan like Baechu Kimchi (napa cabbage kimchi, page 42).

닭갈비 DAK GALBI
SPICY MARINATED CHICKEN

Serves 4 / Prep time: 20 minutes, plus 4 to 24 hours to marinate /
Cook time: 20 minutes

Dak galbi is related to spicy Dwaeji Bulgogi (spicy marinated pork, page 27), but it can be made a little saucier from all the vegetables that are usually grilled with it (see the prep tips). For this recipe, I focus on the chicken, but feel free to include cabbage, carrots, and onions to round it out.

8 boneless, skinless
   chicken thighs
2 tablespoons gochujang
2 tablespoons coarse
   gochugaru flakes
2 tablespoons
   minced garlic
2 teaspoons peeled
   grated fresh ginger
2 tablespoons toasted
   sesame oil
2 tablespoons lightly
   packed dark
   brown sugar
2 tablespoons soy sauce
1 teaspoon kosher salt

1. Slice the chicken into thin, even pieces, about ½ inch thick, and remove any unwanted fat.

2. In a large bowl, whisk together the gochujang, gochugaru, garlic, ginger, oil, brown sugar, soy sauce, and salt. Add the chicken pieces and combine until the marinade is evenly incorporated. Cover and refrigerate the bowl and let the chicken marinate for at least 4 hours, although 24 hours is best.

3. When you're ready to grill, shake off and discard any excess marinade from the chicken. Grill the pieces over medium-high heat for about 10 minutes per side, making sure not to move them around too much so that you can get some browning, until the juice runs clear and there is no pink in the center.

PAIRS WELL WITH: Dak galbi is delicious with a little bit of Pa Muchim (green onion salad, page 48).

PREP TIPS: You can leave the chicken thighs whole if you like. Also, if you want to add vegetables, mix 1 inch pieces of carrot, cabbage, and onion (about 2 cups total) into the marinated chicken right before spooning it onto a grill pan over medium-high heat. Add 10 minutes to the cook time.

돼지불고기 DWAEJI BULGOGI
SPICY MARINATED PORK

Serves 4 / Prep time: 20 minutes, plus 30 minutes to freeze and 4 to 24 hours to marinate / **Cook time:** 10 to 15 minutes

Salty and sweet beef bulgogi is well-known, but this spicy pork version is one of my favorites on the KBBQ table. Pork shoulder is the cut typically used for dwaeji bulgogi, but you can use any tender piece; pork loin is great. This dish showcases gochujang, which is earthy and sharply intense. The marinade balances each bite, and the ginger adds spiciness and complexity, leveled out with a bit of sweetness.

2 pounds boneless pork shoulder

¼ cup gochujang

2 tablespoons coarse gochugaru flakes

2 tablespoons packed dark brown sugar

2 tablespoons minced garlic

2 teaspoons peeled minced fresh ginger

2 tablespoons toasted sesame oil

2 tablespoons soy sauce

2 teaspoons kosher salt

PAIRS WELL WITH:
Dwaeji bulgogi is full flavored, so it goes well with Pa Muchim (green onion salad, page 48) or any other banchan that isn't as spicy.

1. Freeze the pork for about 30 minutes to make it easier to handle. Once it is frozen, slice the pork across the grain into thin, even pieces, about ⅛ inch thick.

2. In a medium bowl, whisk together the gochujang, gochugaru, brown sugar, garlic, ginger, oil, soy sauce, and salt. Add the sliced pork and combine until the marinade is evenly incorporated. Cover and refrigerate the bowl and let the pork marinate for at least 4 hours, although 24 hours is best.

3. When you're ready to grill, shake off and discard any excess marinade from the pork. Grill the dwaeji bulgogi over medium-high heat for 5 to 7 minutes per side, or until bits of char start to show.

MAKE-AHEAD TIP: Once the pork slices are in the marinade, the dwaeji bulgogi can be stored in the freezer for up to three months. Thaw the meat in the refrigerator for one day before cooking.

맥적 MAEKJEOK
DOENJANG MARINATED PORK

Serves 4 / Prep time: 15 minutes, plus 30 minutes to freeze and 4 to 24 hours to marinate / **Cook time:** 10 to 15 minutes

This recipe is a descendant of one of the oldest meat-marinating styles in Korea. Before chiles were brought to the country, doenjang, a fermented bean paste made out of soybeans and salt brine, was used to flavor and preserve whatever cut of pork was on hand. This was once a dish served only to royalty, but now we all get to soak up its goodness.

1 pound pork loin

2 tablespoons doenjang

2 tablespoons
  plum syrup

1 tablespoon soy sauce

1 tablespoon rice vinegar

1 tablespoon
  minced garlic

1 tablespoon coarse
  ground black pepper

1. Freeze the pork for about 30 minutes to make it easier to handle. Once it is frozen, slice the pork across the grain into thin, even pieces, about ⅛ inch thick.

2. In a medium bowl, whisk together the doenjang, plum syrup, soy sauce, vinegar, garlic, and pepper. Add the sliced pork, and combine until the marinade is evenly incorporated. Cover and refrigerate the bowl and let the pork marinate for at least 4 hours, although 24 hours is best.

3. When you're ready to grill, shake off and discard any excess marinade from the pork. Grill the pork loin over medium-high heat for 5 to 7 minutes per side, or until bits of char start to show.

PAIRS WELL WITH: Here's a perfect combination: Put a piece of maekjeok into a kkaennip leaf and a Ssam Mu (marinated radish wraps, page 50), and top it with Pa Muchim (green onion salad, page 48).

오리구이 ORI GUI
MARINATED DUCK

Serves 4 / Prep time: 20 minutes, plus 30 minutes to freeze and 4 to 24 hours to marinate / **Cook time:** 8 minutes

If you've mastered all of the popular and traditional Korean barbecue meats already and want to try something new, duck is a good bet. This extra-meaty, fatty bird (especially compared to its poultry counterpart) has extra layers of flavor that work wonderfully with a soy-forward marinade. It may not be a common Korean protein, but duck is a great addition to the KBBQ table.

2 pounds white Peking
   duck breast
1 medium Fuji apple,
   cored and coarsely
   chopped into
   2-inch pieces
3 tablespoons soy sauce
2 tablespoons
   rice vinegar
1 tablespoon plum syrup
3 large garlic cloves
1 (1-inch) knob
   ginger, peeled

1. Freeze the duck breasts for about 30 minutes to make them easier to handle. Once they are frozen, slice the duck breasts across the grain into thin, even pieces, about ⅛ inch thick. Place the pieces into a medium bowl, and set aside.

2. In a food processor, blend the apple, soy sauce, vinegar, plum syrup, garlic, and ginger together until smooth. Pour the marinade into the bowl with the duck pieces and combine until evenly incorporated. Cover and refrigerate the bowl and let the duck pieces marinate for at least 4 hours, although 24 hours is best.

3. When you're ready to grill, shake off and discard any excess marinade from the duck. Grill the duck over medium-high heat for about 4 minutes per side, until you start to see caramelization.

PAIRS WELL WITH: Eat this succulent piece of duck with a crisp Ssam Mu (marinated radish wraps, page 50). The drippings from this grilling session are perfect to use for the Bokkeumbap (fried rice, page 74) at the end of the meal.

새우구이 **SAEU GUI**

MARINATED SHRIMP

Serves 4 / Prep time: 15 minutes, plus 2 hours to marinate / **Cook time:** 4 minutes

Even though shrimp is not part of a traditional Korean barbecue, it has earned its spot in the lineup because it cooks quickly and holds on to a marinade quite well. Shrimp are also perfect for skewers if you're grilling on a larger stand-alone grill instead of on the tabletop. You can eat the shells, but if that's too much texture for you, remove them before you marinate.

1 pound large raw shrimp

¼ cup soy sauce

2 tablespoons lightly packed dark brown sugar

1 tablespoon coarse gochugaru flakes

2 tablespoons minced garlic

1. Peel the shrimp, if desired. Devein the shrimp by lightly cutting the top of the shrimp from head to tail and removing the dark line. Rinse under cold water, and pat dry with paper towels.

2. In a large bowl, whisk together the soy sauce, brown sugar, gochugaru, and garlic. Add the shrimp and combine until the marinade is evenly incorporated. Cover and refrigerate the bowl and let the shrimp marinate for no more than 2 hours.

3. When you're ready to grill, shake off and discard any excess marinade from the shrimp. Grill the shrimp over medium-high heat for about 2 minutes per side. The middle of the shrimp should be opaque.

PAIRS WELL WITH: Take one whole shrimp and wrap it in a lettuce ssam bundle with a little bit of Ssamjang (fermented soybean and chili dipping sauce, page 36) and Baechu Kimchi (napa cabbage kimchi, page 42).

PREP TIP: Make sure not to marinate the shrimp for more than two hours or it can get gummy.

오징어구이 **OJINGEO GUI**
SPICY MARINATED SQUID

Serves 4 / Prep time: 20 minutes, plus 2 hours to marinate / **Cook time:** 6 minutes

Preparing a piece of squid can be cumbersome, so I usually opt for frozen pieces that already have the body and tentacles separated and cleaned. As long as you don't overcook it on the grill, the squid will have a wonderful texture that you can't achieve with any of the other proteins. Usually, this dish is prepared with a spicy side, but the sweetness from the plum syrup will balance it out.

2 pounds squid, thawed
  if frozen, cleaned,
  body and tentacles
  separated

2 tablespoons gochujang

1 tablespoon coarse
  gochugaru flakes

1 tablespoon
  minced garlic

1 tablespoon plum syrup

1 tablespoon toasted
  sesame oil

1 tablespoon rice vinegar

2 teaspoons kosher salt

1. Pat the squid dry with a paper towel.

2. In a large bowl, whisk together the gochujang, gochugaru, garlic, plum syrup, oil, vinegar, and salt. Add the squid and combine until the marinade is evenly incorporated. Cover and refrigerate the bowl and let the squid marinate for 2 hours.

3. When you're ready to grill, shake off and discard any excess marinade from the squid. Grill the squid over medium-high heat for about 3 minutes per side. The middle of the squid should be opaque. Use scissors to cut the squid into bite-size pieces.

PAIRS WELL WITH: To taste the full flavor and texture of the squid, eat a bite just with rice first, then add your favorite banchan.

TOFU BULGOGI

Serves 4 / Prep time: 30 minutes, plus 6 hours to freeze, 24 hours to thaw, and 4 to 24 hours to marinate / **Cook time:** 10 minutes

This recipe, though not traditional to Korean barbecue, holds true to KBBQ flavors and allows everyone, even vegans, to partake. The saltiness of the soy sauce complements the buttery, toasted sesame oil, leaving just enough room for the garlic to make an appearance. Firm pressed tofu is the perfect vessel for this marinade. Yes, preparing the tofu takes some time, but by completely freezing the tofu block first, then thawing it, then marinating it, you remove all the moisture to create the perfect dense texture.

2 (14-ounce) packages
   firm tofu

½ cup soy sauce

3 tablespoons toasted
   sesame oil

2 tablespoons
   minced garlic

2 tablespoons
   rice vinegar

1 tablespoon coarse
   ground black pepper

PAIRS WELL WITH: Put this tofu bulgogi in a ssam bundle with Baechu Kimchi (napa cabbage kimchi, page 42), Ssamjang (fermented soybean and chili dipping sauce, page 36), and Pa Muchim (green onion salad, page 48).

1. Drain the water from the tofu packages, but leave the tofu in the packages. Place the packages in the freezer for at least 6 hours (or overnight), until completely frozen. After they are completely frozen, thaw them in the refrigerator for about 24 hours. Once thawed, remove the tofu from the packaging and use a clean kitchen towel to soak up any excess moisture. Cut the tofu into 1-inch cubes.

2. In a medium bowl, whisk together the soy sauce, oil, garlic, vinegar, and pepper. Add the tofu and combine until the marinade is evenly incorporated. Cover and refrigerate the bowl and let the tofu marinate for at least 4 hours, although 24 hours is best.

3. When you're ready to grill, shake off and discard any excess marinade from the tofu. Grill the tofu over high heat for about 5 minutes per side, until both sides are golden brown and the edges have a slight crisp to them. Eat this straight off the grill, or transfer it to a large platter if serving it as a banchan.

JACKFRUIT BULGOGI

Serves 4 / Prep time: 20 minutes, plus 1 to 4 hours to marinate /
Cook time: 15 minutes

If you're looking for a plant-based main protein for KBBQ, jackfruit is a definite winner. It holds up quite well to the bulgogi marinade and is delightfully substantial in a lettuce wrap. Understandably, a lot of vegans are not looking for a meaty texture, but you'll be able to fool your meat-eating friends with jackfruit because it resembles the texture and flavor of pulled pork when cooked.

2 (20-ounce) cans
  jackfruit in brine (see
  prep tip)
2 tablespoons soy sauce
2 tablespoons
  plum syrup
2 tablespoons
  minced garlic
2 teaspoons kosher salt
2 teaspoons coarse
  ground black pepper
1 teaspoon peeled
  grated fresh ginger
1 teaspoon toasted
  sesame oil

1. Drain the jackfruit, rinse it well with cold water, and wring out as much water as possible. Cut the jackfruit through the core into roughly 1-inch pieces.

2. In a large bowl, whisk together the soy sauce, plum syrup, garlic, salt, pepper, ginger, and oil. Add the jackfruit and combine until the marinade is evenly incorporated. Cover and refrigerate the bowl and let the jackfruit marinate for at least 1 hour, although 4 hours is best.

3. When you're ready to grill, shake off and discard any excess marinade from the jackfruit. On a grill pan over high heat, grill the jackfruit for about 15 minutes, tossing every few minutes, until the ends are crispy.

PREP TIP: When buying the jackfruit, make sure you purchase cans of young, green jackfruit rather than the ripe, yellow kind that is generally bathed in syrup.

PAIRS WELL WITH: Wrap this jackfruit bulgogi in a traditional ssam of red leaf lettuce and Baechu Kimchi (napa cabbage kimchi, page 42).

GOCHUJANG EGGPLANT GUI

Serves 4 / Prep time: 20 minutes, plus 1 hour to dry brine the eggplant /
Cook time: 8 minutes

Veggie eaters and meat lovers alike will enjoy the unique flavors of this nontra-ditional KBBQ addition. Eggplant is a little high maintenance, but it is definitely worth it. Don't skip the salting step: This draws the moisture out of the egg-plant and firms it up before it's bathed in the spicy, umami-rich pepper paste. The sweetness in the marinade will help char the eggplant pieces when they're quickly grilled, adding extra flavor to every bite.

2 Chinese eggplants (see prep tip)

2 tablespoons kosher salt

¼ cup gochujang

2 tablespoons lightly packed dark brown sugar

2 tablespoons soy sauce

2 tablespoons toasted sesame oil

1 tablespoon minced garlic

2 teaspoons peeled grated fresh ginger

PAIRS WELL WITH: Wrap a piece of this gochujang eggplant gui in a perilla leaf and dip it in some Gireumjang (salt and sesame oil dipping sauce, page 6).

1. Line a rimmed baking sheet with paper towels or a clean kitchen towel. Cut the eggplants into 1-inch-thick rounds. Place the eggplant rounds on the prepared baking sheet and sprinkle the salt evenly over both sides of each round. Set aside in the refrigerator for 1 hour to draw some moisture out.

2. In a medium bowl, whisk together the gochu-jang, brown sugar, soy sauce, oil, garlic, and ginger. When the eggplant is ready, add it to the bowl without removing the salt and gently coat all of the pieces in the marinade.

3. When you're ready to grill, shake off and discard any excess marinade from the egg-plant. On a grill pan over high heat, grill the eggplant for about 4 minutes per side, making sure the eggplant is browning but still slightly firm. Eggplant can get mushy very quickly, so make sure not to overcook it.

PREP TIP: Chinese eggplants are slender, about 7 inches long, and have fewer seeds compared to the wider Italian eggplants. If you can't find the Chinese variety, it's okay to use the Italian, just make sure to cut the larger rounds in half so they are bite-size.

OYSTER MUSHROOM BULGOGI

Serves 4 / Prep time: 15 minutes, plus 30 minutes to marinate / **Cook time:** 4 minutes

Here's another option for those vegetarians at your table. This one is quick and easy and oh so delicious. You can use any mushroom you'd like for this recipe, but using hand-torn oyster mushrooms will create lovely nooks and crannies for the bulgogi marinade to burrow into. Since fungi are delicate, it takes only a brief time to flavor the pieces.

1 pound oyster
  mushrooms

2 tablespoons
  minced garlic

¼ cup soy sauce

2 tablespoons toasted
  sesame oil

2 tablespoons
  plum syrup

1 tablespoon coarse
  ground black pepper

1. Remove any dirt from the oyster mushrooms with a damp paper towel. Cut off the root ends that connect each mushroom. Using your hands, tear the mushrooms into roughly 1-inch-long pieces.

2. In a medium bowl, whisk together the garlic, soy sauce, oil, plum syrup, and pepper. Add the torn mushroom pieces and combine until the marinade is evenly incorporated. Set aside for 30 minutes to marinate.

3. When you're ready to grill, shake off and discard any excess marinade from the mushrooms. On a grill pan over high heat, grill the mushrooms for 2 minutes, letting them remain undisturbed to create a char, then flip the mushrooms and cook for 2 minutes more. Eat this bulgogi hot off the grill, or transfer it to a large platter if serving it as a banchan.

PAIRS WELL WITH: Bundle a piece of Oyster Mushroom Bulgogi in a lettuce wrap with some Pa Muchim (green onion salad, page 48) or your banchan of choice.

쌈장 SSAMJANG
FERMENTED SOYBEAN AND CHILI DIPPING SAUCE

Makes 1 cup / Prep time: 10 minutes

Ssamjang is a thick, spicy paste that will give you a savory umami explosion when you dollop some into your wrap. This versatile dipping sauce is primarily used in ssam wraps, but it can be eaten with a freshly cut cucumber or carrot spear, too.

½ cup doenjang

3 tablespoons gochujang

1 tablespoon
 minced garlic

1 tablespoon toasted
 sesame oil

1 tablespoon fish sauce

1 tablespoon rice vinegar

1 teaspoon coarse
 gochugaru flakes

Pinch sesame seeds

In a small bowl, thoroughly combine the doenjang, gochujang, garlic, oil, fish sauce, vinegar, gochugaru, and sesame seeds. Serve the sauce at room temperature.

MAKE-AHEAD TIP: This sauce can be made ahead of time and kept covered in the refrigerator for months. Before serving, bring it to room temperature and add a splash of toasted sesame oil if the ssamjang needs to loosen up. Because this keeps so well, it's smart to triple the recipe to keep on hand.

PAIRS WELL WITH: Grab a red lettuce leaf, smear on a small dollop of ssamjang, add a piece of grilled Bulgogi (thinly sliced marinated beef, page 22), and top it with a little Baechu Kimchi (napa cabbage kimchi, page 42) for a wonderful ssam bundle.

새우젓장 SAEUJEOT JANG
SPICY FERMENTED SHRIMP SAUCE

Makes ½ cup / Prep time: 10 minutes

The main ingredient in this sauce is saeujeot, salted fermented shrimp, which boasts a sharper taste than most other fermented seafoods. The shrimp give this dip deep umami flavors. Use this dipping sauce only with main proteins that are not marinated (see Presliced, Unseasoned Cuts of Meat, page 39), otherwise the flavors will be overwhelming.

1 green onion,
  finely chopped
1 small Fresno chile,
  stemmed and
  finely chopped
1 teaspoon minced garlic
2 teaspoons saeujeot
2 tablespoons toasted
  sesame oil
1 teaspoon coarse
  gochugaru flakes
1 teaspoon sesame seeds

In a small bowl, thoroughly combine the green onion, chile, garlic, saeujeot, oil, gochugaru, and sesame seeds. Serve the sauce at room temperature.

PAIRS WELL WITH: This sauce is a lovely salty addition to Samgyeopsal (pork belly, page 39).

MAKE-AHEAD TIP: Saeujeot Jang can be made a week ahead of time and stored covered in the refrigerator. If you wait to add the green onions until you're ready to serve (so they don't get mushy), you can keep this sauce in the refrigerator for up to a month.

GREEN ONION AND VINEGAR SAUCE

Makes 1 cup / Prep time: 10 minutes

Since KBBQ can have a lot of heavy notes, I created this dipping sauce to brighten up heavily marinated proteins. The vinegar gives a refreshing splash to a ssam bundle, and the green onion bits also give great texture. If you're skipping the wrap, you can drizzle this sauce on top of a protein right before you eat it with a spoonful of rice.

2 green onions,
  finely chopped

¼ cup rice vinegar

1 tablespoon toasted
  sesame oil

1 teaspoon white sugar

½ teaspoon kosher salt

½ teaspoon
  sesame seeds

In a small bowl, thoroughly combine the green onions, vinegar, oil, sugar, salt, and sesame seeds. Serve the sauce at room temperature.

PAIRS WELL WITH: Drizzle this sauce onto a piece of marinated Deungsim (marinated strip steak, page 24) sitting on top of rice. It is mouthwateringly good.

PRESLICED, UNSEASONED CUTS OF MEAT

Along with all of the marinated options for the main protein, Korean barbecue features an assortment of presliced, unmarinated meats. A Korean grocery store will have these already cut and set out for purchase, but you can also ask any butcher to thinly slice the cuts of meat for you. Sometimes these will be frozen after slicing so they turn into a curled shape. These can stay frozen until you're ready to grill and will still cook quickly with just a couple of extra minutes. When these slices are hot off the grill, you can dip them in the Gireumjang (salt and sesame oil dipping sauce, page 6) and eat them with any of the banchans.

SAMGYEOPSAL 삼겹살 PORK BELLY

Samgyeopsal has a luxurious ratio of fat to meat that perfectly pairs with any banchan that is very well-fermented, like Baechu Kimchi (napa cabbage kimchi, page 42). Look for pork belly that is either (1) precut into paper-thin slices so it crisps up very quickly, or (2) thick cut so that it gives more chew and renders out more fat. Thick-cut samgyeopsal is particularly great when you're cooking it alongside vegetables, which will soak up the pork fat and become so much more flavorful.

HANGJEONGSAL 항정살 PORK JOWL

If you're looking for more of an equal ratio of fat and meat, hangjeongsal is the cut for you. The pork jowl pieces are meatier than samgyeopsal but still retain maximum flavor from the marbling. Eat hangjeongsal in a ssam bundle with rice and a banchan.

CHADOL BAGI 차돌박이 BEEF BRISKET

This shaved cut of beef shines without any marinade. The thin slices, which can be purchased presliced from the store, cook instantly when they hit the hot grill. The Gireumjang (salt and sesame oil dipping sauce, page 6) and Green Onion and Vinegar Sauce (page 38) were made to go with this paper-thin brisket.

USEOL 우설 BEEF TONGUE

Beef tongue offers one of the most tender bites of beef you can have. Sliced just as thin as chadol bagi, it'll be ready to jump into a lettuce wrap before other proteins have even had a chance to begin sizzling.

SIGEUMCHI NAMUL,
SEASONED SPINACH; PAGE 57

BAECHU GEOTJEORI,
FRESH KIMCHI; PAGE 44

OI MUCHIM,
SPICY CUCUMBER SALAD; PAGE 47

SIDES (BANCHANS)

배추김치 BAECHU KIMCHI
NAPA CABBAGE KIMCHI

Makes 1 gallon / Prep time: 40 minutes, plus 4 hours to dry brine the cabbage /
Fermentation time: 3 weeks

This is the kimchi everyone thinks of when they hear the word kimchi. *Nevertheless, despite its ubiquity, every restaurant's and every household's baechu kimchi will vary in taste. Over time, you'll figure out the combination you like best, whether it's sweeter, more seafood-centered, or extra pungent from longer fermentation. Use either Korean coarse sea salt or any extra-coarse kosher salt to avoid making the kimchi overly salty. The anchovy fillets are my personal touch.*

½ cup Korean coarse sea
   salt or extra-coarse
   kosher salt, for
   dry brining

2 (2- to 2½-pound)
   heads napa cabbage,
   quartered

1 large Fuji apple, cored
   and coarsely chopped

1 medium yellow onion,
   coarsely chopped

1 (2-inch) knob
   ginger, peeled and
   coarsely chopped

½ cup garlic cloves,
   peeled, whole

3 tablespoons fish sauce

4 anchovy fillets

1 cup coarse
   gochugaru flakes

2 medium carrots, grated

10 Asian chives or
   5 green onions, cut into
   1-inch pieces

1. In an extra-large bowl, lightly sprinkle the salt on each cabbage leaf by lifting each leaf and making sure the salt gets right down to the root. Set aside on the counter in a cool area for 4 hours. The cabbage leaves should be pliable but still have a crunch. Rinse the salt off the leaves and shake off any excess water.

2. In a food processor, combine the apple, onion, ginger, garlic, fish sauce, and anchovy fillets and pulse until most of it is broken up. Add the gochugaru to the food processor and pulse until it turns into a rough paste.

3. In an extra-large bowl, mix together the paste, grated carrots, and chives. Using your hands, spread the paste on each individual cabbage leaf, making sure to get all the way to the core and rubbing the paste all over the cabbage head so every part has the paste on it.

4. Place the paste-coated cabbage in a BPA-free plastic or glass container, pressing the cabbage down to get rid of air bubbles. Cover the container with a lid and leave it on the counter in a cool area for a few days to activate the fermentation (see the kkakdugi prep tip on page 46). When you start to see small bubbles forming in the brine, store the container in the refrigerator for about three weeks, opening the lid once a week to let trapped air out, until fully fermented.

5. Cut the kimchi into 1-inch pieces when you're ready to serve.

PREP TIPS: You can cut the cabbage head into bite-size pieces at the outset, salt them, then mix the pieces with the paste before fermentation. This style is called mak-kimchi. *Mak* 막 translates to roughly or haphazardly because it's not as labor intensive. The mak-kimchi cabbage pieces will not be as crunchy as the kimchi you'll get using the method in this recipe. Also, the fermentation time on the counter could take only two days in a warm kitchen or up to five or six days in a chilly kitchen.

MAKE-AHEAD TIP: This kimchi can be kept in the refrigerator for a very long time. As long as the kimchi isn't moldy, you can eat it. The oldest kimchi I've eaten was fermented for a year.

PAIRS WELL WITH: It's hard to pick just one or even a few things that baechu kimchi pairs well with (everything works), but my favorite way to eat it is with something that either has deep umami like Galbi (marinated short ribs, page 23) or is buttery in fat like Samgyeopsal (pork belly, page 39). And don't forget the rice.

겉절이 BAECHU GEOTJEORI
FRESH KIMCHI

Serves 4 / Prep time: 40 minutes, plus 1 hour to dry brine the cabbage

Baechu geotjeori is called fresh kimchi because it does not ferment. It's quicker and easier to make, and although it does not have the depth of flavor of fermented kimchi, it is lighter and crisper. This recipe adds more flavor to the paste, giving it a fresh punch that can be enjoyed right away. You can skip the salting step if you prefer a crunchier texture.

¼ cup Korean coarse sea salt or extra-coarse kosher salt, for dry brining, plus more as needed

½ (1-pound) head napa cabbage

1 small Fuji apple, cored and coarsely chopped

1 small yellow onion, coarsely chopped

1 (1-inch) knob ginger, peeled and coarsely chopped

½ cup garlic cloves, peeled, whole

2 tablespoons fish sauce

3 tablespoons white sugar

½ cup coarse gochugaru flakes

1 small carrot, grated

5 Asian chives or 2 green onions, cut into 1-inch pieces

1. In an extra-large bowl, lightly sprinkle the salt on each cabbage leaf by lifting each leaf and making sure the salt gets right down to the root. Set aside on the counter in a cool area for 1 hour. The cabbage leaves should be pliable but still have a crunch. Rinse the salt off the leaves and shake off any excess water.

2. In a food processor, combine the apple, onion, ginger, garlic, fish sauce, and sugar and pulse until most of it is broken up. Add the gochugaru to the food processor and pulse until it turns into a rough paste.

3. In a large bowl, mix together the paste, grated carrots, and chives. Using your hands, spread the paste on each individual cabbage leaf, making sure to get all the way to the core and rubbing the paste all over the cabbage head so every part has the paste on it. Break off a small piece to see if more salt is needed, then add salt to taste.

4. Cut the cabbage into 1-inch pieces or long strips and serve on a small platter.

MAKE-AHEAD TIP: Even though baechu geotjeori is made to be eaten fresh, you can make it a day ahead of time.

PAIRS WELL WITH: Because baechu geotjeori is not fermented, I like to eat it with dishes that are deep in flavor like Maekjeok (doenjang marinated pork, page 28) or even other banchans like Gamja Jorim (sweet braised potatoes, page 52).

깍두기 KKAKDUGI

RADISH KIMCHI

Serves 4 / Prep time: 15 minutes, plus 30 minutes to dry brine the cabbage /
Fermentation time: 2 weeks

*Kkakdugi is a beloved kimchi for people who like a little more sweetness and
crunch, and it's also for anyone who is looking for easy-to-make kimchi. Grab
mu (Korean radish) during the cooler months because they will be sweeter.*

2 tablespoons kosher salt

1 tablespoon white sugar

1 (1-pound) Korean
  radish, cut into
  small cubes

3 tablespoons coarse
  gochugaru flakes

2 tablespoons
  minced garlic

1 tablespoon fish sauce

PREP TIP: The ideal temperature for fermentation
to start is 68°F. Warmer
kitchens will speed up fermentation. To make sure
that your batch doesn't
get moldy on the counter,
check it daily for the fermentation bubbles.

1. In a large bowl, mix the salt and sugar with
   the radish pieces. Set aside for 30 minutes.

2. Without rinsing the radish, drain and discard
   the liquid. Mix in the gochugaru, garlic, and
   fish sauce. Taste and adjust the spiciness and
   sweetness to your liking.

3. Transfer the mixture to a glass or BPA-free
   plastic container, pressing the kkakdugi down
   to get rid of any air bubbles. Cover the container with a lid and leave it on the counter
   in a cool area for a few days to activate the
   fermentation. When you start to see small
   bubbles forming in the brine, store the container in the refrigerator for about two weeks,
   opening the lid once a week to let trapped air
   out, until fully fermented. (You can also taste
   your batch each week to note the difference
   until it's fermented to your liking.)

4. When you're ready to serve, spoon the kkakdugi into a small bowl.

PAIRS WELL WITH: Kkakdugi has a lovely crunch and
sweetness, so any of the Presliced, Unseasoned Cuts of
Meat (page 39) will create a delicious bite, especially with
a spoonful of rice.

오이무침 OI MUCHIM
SPICY CUCUMBER SALAD

Serves 4 / Prep time: 15 minutes, plus 1 hour to dry brine the cucumbers

Oi muchim is a crowd-pleaser. The fresh cucumber brings a joyful crunch to any of the marinated proteins. If you're not used to kimchi, oi muchim is a great gateway salad because it's not fermented but still has a nice punch of flavor. It's best to use Korean cucumbers because they have thin skin and small seeds, but you can substitute Persian cucumbers in a pinch.

5 Korean cucumbers, cut into ¼-inch slices

1 tablespoon kosher salt, for dry brining

1 small white onion, thinly sliced

1 Fresno chile, seeded and coarsely chopped

1 medium carrot, julienned

2 tablespoons minced garlic

2 tablespoons coarse gochugaru flakes

2 tablespoons toasted sesame oil

2 tablespoons rice vinegar

1 tablespoon fish sauce

2 teaspoons lightly packed dark brown sugar

½ teaspoon sesame seeds

1. In a strainer, toss the cucumber pieces in the salt. Place the strainer in a bowl to catch the excess water being pulled out. Set aside for 1 hour.

2. Rinse the salt off the cucumber pieces and pat dry with a paper towel. Discard any liquid that was drawn out of the cucumbers.

3. In a large mixing bowl, combine the cucumber pieces with the onion, chile, carrot, garlic, gochugaru, oil, vinegar, fish sauce, and brown sugar. Mix well, evenly coating the vegetables.

4. Garnish the salad with sesame seeds and serve in a small bowl.

MAKE-AHEAD TIP: Oi muchim is best eaten fresh, but you can make it ahead of time, and it will last in the refrigerator for a week. More moisture will emerge from it, but this liquid tastes delicious on rice, so don't toss it out.

PAIRS WELL WITH: Oi Muchim is a must-have because people like to eat it on its own or with Dwaeji Bulgogi (spicy marinated pork, page 27) to cool down the spicy pork.

파무침 PA MUCHIM

GREEN ONION SALAD

Serves 4 / Prep time: 15 minutes

Pa muchim is a great companion for grilled pork or anything else that has lots of delicious, buttery fat. The dressing gives this banchan a fresher zing than fermented kimchi, and the green onions help cut through any heaviness in your ssam bundle.

**2 tablespoons
rice vinegar**

**1 tablespoon toasted
sesame oil**

**2 teaspoons coarse
gochugaru flakes**

2 teaspoons fish sauce

1 teaspoon sesame seeds

**1 cup ice, plus cold water
as needed**

8 green onions

PAIRS WELL WITH: You'll often see pa muchim served with Samgyeopsal (pork belly, page 39) because the onion flavors add a wonderful seasoning to the pork belly.

MAKE-AHEAD TIP: You can make the dressing a few days ahead of time, and store it in the refrigerator until the green onion pieces are ready to be dressed.

1. In a small bowl, combine the vinegar, oil, gochugaru, fish sauce, and sesame seeds. Taste for saltiness and add more fish sauce, if needed. Set aside until ready to serve.

2. Fill a medium bowl with the ice and cold water. Cut off and discard the roots of the green onions. Starting from the white side, cut the green onions at a sharp angle to make 3-inch slivers. Immediately place the sliced pieces into the bowl of ice water. There should be enough water to submerge the onion pieces. Set the bowl aside for a couple of minutes.

3. Remove the onion pieces from the bowl of water, shaking off any excess water, and pat dry with a clean towel. Place the onion pieces into another medium bowl.

4. Right before you are ready to serve, drizzle the dressing all over the green onion slices and gently toss until evenly coated. Serve immediately on a medium serving platter because the pa muchim will start to wilt as soon as the dressing is added.

PREP TIP: You can use a scallion slicer to get curly pieces of green onion.

상추겉절이 SANGCHU GEOTJEORI
KOREAN LETTUCE SALAD

Serves 4 / Prep time: 15 minutes

This bowl of leafy greens is the Korean equivalent to a house salad. Similar to Baechu Geotjeori (fresh kimchi, page 44), this dish isn't fermented and offers a fresh, light crunch to your meal. You can add more vegetables, like bell pepper, carrot, and purple cabbage, or you can keep it simple by adding the dressing to crisp greens. Though red leaf lettuce is most commonly used, you can switch it out for Bibb or Boston lettuce.

For the dressing

1 tablespoon rice vinegar

1 tablespoon toasted
  sesame oil

1 teaspoon coarse
  gochugaru flakes

1 teaspoon garlic powder

1 teaspoon coarse
  ground black pepper

1 teaspoon kosher salt

For the salad

1 head red leaf lettuce,
  coarsely chopped into
  1-inch pieces

1 small yellow onion,
  thinly sliced

1. **To make the dressing:** In a small bowl, whisk together the vinegar, oil, gochugaru, garlic powder, pepper, and salt.

2. **To make the salad:** Just before serving, in a serving bowl, combine the lettuce, onion, and dressing. Toss the salad to evenly incorporate the dressing and serve.

MAKE-AHEAD TIP: You can make the dressing a week ahead of time and keep it in the refrigerator. But remember to dress the salad right before you're ready to serve so it doesn't wilt.

PAIRS WELL WITH: You can definitely eat this salad on its own, but feel free to take bites of it with the Oyster Mushroom Bulgogi (page 35) to give it some added texture.

쌈무 SSAM MU
MARINATED RADISH WRAPS

Serves 4 / Prep time: 15 minutes, plus 4 hours to marinate

Using a mandoline or knife to slice the mu (Korean radishes) as thin as you can is the key to making them suitable as wraps. The quick marinade helps flavor each slice and makes the texture more pliable. The more flexible the wrap, the easier it is to stuff and close. If you can't find mu, you can replace it with daikon.

½ (½-pound) mu (Korean radish), peeled and cut into paper-thin slices
1 cup rice vinegar
1 tablespoon white sugar
2 teaspoons kosher salt
1 teaspoon garlic powder

1. Place the radish slices in a wide bowl and set it aside.

2. In a small bowl, whisk together the vinegar, sugar, salt, and garlic powder.

3. Pour the mixture over the radish slices, making sure to cover each radish piece. Cover and refrigerate the bowl for 4 hours or more to marinate.

4. When you're ready to serve, remove the radish slices from the brine and place them on a medium serving platter with each piece overlapping each other.

MAKE-AHEAD TIP: Ssam mu can be made a few days ahead of time and stored in the refrigerator for about three days. After that, the mu slices will become quite flexible and won't give you the satisfying crunch.

PAIRS WELL WITH: Ssam mu is made to be used as a wrap just like a lettuce leaf, and it is especially tasty with Samgyeopsal (pork belly, page 39) and Baechu Kimchi (napa cabbage kimchi, page 42).

장아찌 JANGAJJI
PICKLED ONIONS AND CHILES

Serves 4 / Prep time: 15 minutes, plus 24 hours to brine the onions and chiles /
Cook time: 5 minutes

*Jangajji is a quick pickled banchan packed full with flavors from the equal
amounts of soy sauce and vinegar. The onions and chiles will still have a nice
crunch after you add the hot brine to the mix. These are so irresistible it's super
hard to wait the mere 24 hours for these pickled onions and chiles to be ready.*

1 large yellow onion,
 chopped into
 ½-inch chunks

2 jalapeño peppers,
 thinly sliced

4 garlic cloves,
 thinly sliced

½ cup soy sauce

½ cup rice vinegar

½ cup water

¼ cup white sugar

1. In a 32-ounce mason pickling jar with a lid,
 combine the onion, jalapeños, and garlic.

2. In a medium pot over high heat, combine the
 soy sauce, vinegar, water, and sugar and bring
 to a boil. Boil the mixture for 3 minutes, then
 pour the hot brine on top of the vegetables in
 the jar. Let it cool to room temperature.

3. Cover and refrigerate the jar for 24 hours
 before serving. When you're ready to serve,
 scoop the jangajji into a small bowl.

MAKE-AHEAD TIP: Jangajji can be store in the refrigerator for two weeks, during which the flavors will continue
to develop.

PAIRS WELL WITH: The Gochujang Eggplant Gui
(page 34) would be perfect with jangajji because of the
complementary flavors and the added crunch.

감자조림 **GAMJA JORIM**
SWEET BRAISED POTATOES

Serves 4 / Prep time: 15 minutes / **Cook time:** 25 minutes

These potatoes are braised in a sweet and salty bath to infuse maximum flavor. They take a little more time to make, but your patience will be rewarded with these slightly sticky and superbly sweet spuds. You can substitute the Yukon Gold potatoes with sweet potatoes to add some nutrients, or use baby potatoes for a quicker, no-cut option.

½ cup water

3 tablespoons soy sauce

2 tablespoons
plum syrup

2 tablespoons toasted
sesame oil

2 tablespoons
rice vinegar

1 tablespoon lightly
packed dark
brown sugar

1 tablespoon
minced garlic

1 teaspoon kosher salt

2 tablespoons
vegetable oil

1 pound (about 4)
Yukon Gold potatoes,
peeled and cut into
2-inch pieces

½ teaspoon
sesame seeds

1. In a small bowl, combine the water, soy sauce, plum syrup, sesame oil, vinegar, brown sugar, garlic, and salt to make the braising sauce. Set aside.

2. In a large pan, heat the vegetable oil over medium high heat. Add the potatoes and sauté for about 5 minutes, until slightly softened.

3. Increase the heat to high and pour the braising sauce over the potatoes. Bring it to a boil, then turn the heat down to medium-low and cover the pan. Simmer for about 15 minutes, stirring occasionally, until the braising liquid reduces to a syrup and the potatoes are soft.

4. Sprinkle the potatoes with sesame seeds and serve warm or at room temperature on a small serving platter.

MAKE-AHEAD TIP: Gamja jorim can be made a week ahead of time and stored in the refrigerator. Bring the dish up to room temperature before serving.

PAIRS WELL WITH: The sweet and savory potatoes are so delicious with just a spoonful of rice. This is also one of my favorite banchans to eat with other banchans like Baechu Kimchi (napa cabbage kimchi, page 42).

감자샐러드 **GAMJA SALAD**
KOREAN POTATO SALAD

Serves 4 / Prep time: 40 minutes / **Cook time:** 20 minutes

*For people unfamiliar with KBBQ, potato salad is usually the banchan that con-
fuses them the most because it's such a common American barbecue side dish.
But all questions quickly disappear when they taste the fluffy, sweet Korean version. This is no Fourth of July potluck potato salad swimming in mayo. This
version has a lot of texture, tang, and taste, featuring fresh apples and cucumbers.*

1 cup ice, plus cold water
   as needed

1 pound (about 4)
   Yukon Gold potatoes,
   peeled and cut into
   1-inch pieces

2 large eggs

1 small Fuji apple, cored
   and finely chopped

2 Persian cucumbers,
   finely chopped

½ cup mayonnaise

1 tablespoon white sugar

½ teaspoon kosher salt

MAKE-AHEAD TIP: You
can make gamja salad one
day ahead of time and
store it in a covered container in the refrigerator.

PAIRS WELL WITH:
Try this banchan with a
spoonful of rice and you'll
be pleasantly surprised by
how well they go together.

1. Fill a medium bowl with the ice and cold
   water. Set aside.

2. In a large pot over high heat, cover the potato
   pieces with water by 1 inch. Bring the potatoes
   to a boil, then add the eggs. Let the eggs boil
   for 10 minutes, then transfer them to the bowl
   of ice water. Continue to boil the potatoes for
   10 minutes more, until the pieces are tender
   but not mushy. Transfer the potatoes to a
   baking sheet or large plate and spread them
   out in a thin layer. Let the potatoes cool for at
   least 30 minutes.

3. Once the eggs have cooled, peel and roughly
   chop them into ½-inch pieces.

4. In a large bowl, combine the cooled potatoes and eggs with the apple, cucumber,
   mayonnaise, sugar, and salt. Gently fold the
   ingredients together until everything is thoroughly combined.

5. Cover and refrigerate the bowl until ready to
   serve, and then spoon the gamja salad into a
   medium serving bowl.

계란찜 GYERANJJIM
STEAMED EGGS

Serves 4 / Prep time: 15 minutes / **Cook time:** 15 minutes

Gyeranjjim is one of the best ways to make an egg luxurious. The ingredient list is very simple, but the technique turns the mixture into a velvety, custardy, casserole-like, light, fluffy delicacy. Traditionally made in a Korean earthenware pot, you can use any heat-safe ramekin to make this dish.

5 large eggs, beaten

1 tablespoon fish sauce

1 cup water, plus more for steaming

1 green onion, thinly sliced, for garnish

1 teaspoon toasted sesame oil

1. In a heat-safe ramekin, whisk together the eggs, fish sauce, and water.

2. Place the ramekin in a medium pot, and add water around the ramekin until it reaches halfway up the ramekin. Cover the pot.

3. Bring the pot to a low simmer over medium-low heat and cook for 10 minutes. Uncover the pot and cook for 2 minutes more, making sure the eggs are set. Using a thick dish towel, quickly remove the ramekin from the pot.

4. Top the eggs with green onions and a drizzle of oil, and serve hot.

PREP TIP: For more flavor, you can switch out the cup of water for any broth and add one teaspoon of Saeujeot Jang (spicy fermented shrimp sauce, page 37) instead of the fish sauce.

PAIRS WELL WITH: Eat these luxurious eggs with rice and any other flavorful banchan like Kkakdugi (radish kimchi, page 46).

두부조림 DUBU JORIM
SPICY BRAISED TOFU

Serves 4 / Prep time: 15 minutes / **Cook time:** 20 minutes

Tofu is common in Korea and a perfect vegetarian option for your KBBQ. This panfried, then braised version soaks up every bit of flavor from the braising sauce, which offers lots of umami and spice. Even though this banchan is wonderful hot, it's just as delicious cold, making it a great candidate to make ahead of time.

1 (14-ounce) package firm tofu, drained (not pressed)

2 tablespoons vegetable oil

3 tablespoons soy sauce

1 tablespoon minced garlic

1 tablespoon coarse gochugaru flakes

1 tablespoon lightly packed dark brown sugar

1 tablespoon rice vinegar

1 tablespoon toasted sesame oil

½ cup water

¼ teaspoon sesame seeds

2 green onions, thinly sliced, for garnish

PAIRS WELL WITH:
Dubu jorim is perfect with rice or a piece of crispy Samgyeopsal (pork belly, page 39).

1. Halve the tofu block lengthwise, then cut it into ½-inch-thick squares. Pat dry with a paper towel.

2. In a large nonstick pan, heat the vegetable oil over medium-high heat. Fry the tofu pieces for about 5 minutes per side, until they're browned on each side.

3. In a small bowl, whisk together the soy sauce, garlic, gochugaru, brown sugar, vinegar, sesame oil, and water.

4. Increase the heat under the tofu to high and add the braising sauce. Bring it to a boil, then reduce the heat to medium-low and cover the pan. Simmer for about 10 minutes, occasionally flipping the tofu pieces, until the braising liquid reduces to a syrup and the tofu pieces are coated. Remove the pan from the heat.

5. Transfer the dubu jorim to a medium serving platter and sprinkle with sesame seeds and green onions to serve.

MAKE-AHEAD TIP: You can make dubu jorim a few days ahead of time. Just make sure to bring it to room temperature before serving.

ROASTED BROCCOLI WITH SWEETENED GOCHUJANG SAUCE

Serves 4 / Prep time: 15 minutes / **Cook time:** 30 minutes

You'll usually see this banchan on a KBBQ restaurant table as plain old steamed broccoli. If you're lucky, it'll be dressed in toasted sesame oil. This recipe steps it up by calling for roasted broccoli to bring out more flavor and those lovely crispy bits on the florets. And I've added this easy, albeit nontraditional, gochujang sauce for even more flavor.

For the broccoli

3 cups (about 1 large head) broccoli florets

2 tablespoons vegetable oil

2 teaspoons kosher salt

For the sauce

2 tablespoons gochujang

2 tablespoons plum syrup

1 tablespoon rice vinegar

1 teaspoon garlic powder

1. **To make the broccoli:** Preheat the oven to 425°F. Line a baking sheet with parchment paper.

2. On the prepared baking sheet, toss the broccoli with the vegetable oil and salt.

3. Roast the broccoli for 30 minutes, or until the edges are crispy.

4. Transfer the broccoli to a serving dish and set it aside.

5. **To make the sauce:** In a small bowl, whisk together the gochujang, plum syrup, vinegar, and garlic powder.

6. Drizzle the sauce on top of the roasted broccoli and serve at room temperature.

MAKE-AHEAD TIP: You can make the gochujang sauce ahead of time and keep it in the refrigerator for as long as you like; the ingredients are not perishable.

PAIRS WELL WITH: This broccoli is delicious with just a spoonful of rice. You could also eat it with Daegujeon (breaded cod fillets, page 64).

시금치나물 SIGEUMCHI NAMUL
SEASONED SPINACH

Serves 4 / Prep time: 15 minutes / **Cook time:** 5 minutes

Spinach is a superfood containing lots of iron, vitamin C, calcium, and magnesium. And sigeumchi namul is a wonderful way to eat a lot of these healthy greens in one bite. This simple banchan is lightly seasoned and quickly blanched, which cooks down the spinach dramatically in size.

2 cups ice

2 cups water

1 pound spinach

1 teaspoon minced garlic

1 tablespoon soy sauce

1 tablespoon toasted sesame oil

1 teaspoon kosher salt

1 teaspoon sesame seeds

1. In a large bowl, combine the ice and water. Set aside.

2. Bring a medium pot of water to a boil over high heat. Add the spinach and cook for 2 minutes, until wilted. Then, using a spider or slotted spoon, immediately transfer the spinach to the ice bath. Let cool for about 30 seconds.

3. Once the spinach is cool, transfer it to a kitchen towel and wring out as much water as possible.

4. In a small bowl, toss the spinach with the garlic, soy sauce, oil, salt, and sesame seeds until incorporated.

5. Place the sigeumchi namul on a small platter and serve.

MAKE-AHEAD TIP: Sigeumchi namul can be made a few days ahead of time and stored in a covered container in the refrigerator. Bring it up to room temperature before serving.

PAIRS WELL WITH: Sigeumchi namul can be eaten with just rice, but I especially like to combine it with Kongnamul Muchim (seasoned soybean sprouts, page 58) to give the bite more texture.

콩나물무침 KONGNAMUL MUCHIM
SEASONED SOYBEAN SPROUTS

Serves 4 / Prep time: 15 minutes

Kongnamul muchim is usually blanched, but my unblanched version is quicker and has a fresher texture. When picking up sprouts for this recipe, make sure to buy the soybean sprouts with hard heads instead of soft mung bean sprouts, which look similar. This kongnamul variety has great texture, giving this banchan a flavorful crunch.

**2 green onions,
  finely chopped**

**1 tablespoon
  minced garlic**

**1 tablespoon toasted
  sesame oil**

1 tablespoon rice vinegar

**1 teaspoon coarse
  gochugaru flakes**

1 teaspoon white sugar

1 teaspoon kosher salt

½ teaspoon sesame seeds

**1 cup soybean sprouts,
  rinsed, picked over, and
  patted dry**

In a medium bowl, mix together the green onions, garlic, oil, vinegar, gochugaru, sugar, salt, and sesame seeds. Add the soybean sprouts, and toss until evenly incorporated. Serve on a small platter.

MAKE-AHEAD TIP: Even though you're eating this fresh instead of blanched, you can make this a few days ahead of time and keep it in a covered container in the refrigerator. The soybean sprouts will slightly wilt, but the flavor will still be delicious.

PAIRS WELL WITH: Eat kongnamul muchim with any dish to which you'd like to add texture, like Tofu Bulgogi (page 32).

어묵볶음 EOMUK BOKKEUM
STIR-FRIED FISH CAKE

Serves 4 / Prep time: 10 minutes / **Cook time:** 10 minutes

Eomuk translates to fish cake in Korean, and it can easily be found in the freezer section of an Asian grocery store. Eomuk come in different shapes, but most come in the form of a flat sheet to make thin, bite-size pieces. Here, you'll stir-fry them in a savory sauce that only gets better the more time it sits. If you want to make this banchan more substantial, just add carrots, bell peppers, and more onion.

2 sheets (½ package or 1 pound) frozen fish cakes, thawed

1 tablespoon soy sauce

1 tablespoon rice vinegar

1 tablespoon toasted sesame oil

2 teaspoons white sugar

1 teaspoon garlic powder

1 teaspoon kosher salt

1 teaspoon coarse ground black pepper

1 tablespoon vegetable oil

½ small yellow onion, thinly sliced

1. Cut the fish cake sheets into 1-by-2-inch rectangles, and set aside.

2. In a small bowl, mix together the soy sauce, vinegar, sesame oil, sugar, garlic powder, salt, and pepper to make the sauce.

3. In a medium pan, heat the vegetable oil over medium-high heat. Sauté the onion for 5 minutes, until it softens. Add the thawed fish cakes and stir for 3 minutes more, until they start to soften up. Add the sauce and stir until evenly incorporated. Turn off the heat and let it rest for 2 minutes.

4. Spoon the eomuk bokkeum into a small serving bowl and serve at room temperature.

PAIRS WELL WITH:
Eomuk bokkeum is best eaten on its own with just a spoonful of rice.

MAKE-AHEAD TIP: Eomuk bokkeum can be made a week in advance and kept in a covered container in the refrigerator. Bring it up to room temperature before serving.

PREP TIP: To make a spicier version, add 1 tablespoon of gochujang and 2 teaspoons of coarse gochugaru flakes to the sauce.

HAEMUL PAJEON, SAVORY SEAFOOD PANCAKES; PAGE 63

SMALL PLATES

밥 BAP
STEAMED SHORT-GRAIN RICE

Serves 4 / Prep time: 5 minutes / **Cook time:** 20 minutes

There are many delicious Korean rice recipes that turn the cooked grains purple or add nutrients with vegetables like peas, but the one I always come back to is plain, short-grained, steamed white rice. The grains offer the perfect canvas for all of the full-flavored dishes you'll be eating with KBBQ. If you eat as much rice as we do in my household, you will want to invest in a rice cooker, which cooks the grains beautifully every time. But knowing how to make rice on the stovetop is a foundational skill. As a rule of thumb, for every ½ cup of raw rice, you will need ¾ of a cup of water.

2 cups short-grain white rice

3 cups water

1. In a medium pot with a lid, rinse the rice with cold water at least 4 times, swirling the water around with your fingers to help release the starch. The water should turn clearer each time you rinse the rice, but it doesn't need to be completely clear. Drain the rice water and add 3 cups of fresh water to the rice in the pot.

2. Bring the rice and water to a boil over high heat, then cover the pot with the lid and reduce the heat to low. Simmer for 10 minutes, then turn off the heat and let the rice steam for 10 minutes more. Don't be tempted to open the lid or the steam will escape.

3. Fluff the rice and serve it right away either in a large serving bowl or in small individual bowls.

PREP TIPS: You can save the starchy water that you get from rinsing the rice to use as a binder in soups like Doenjang Jjigae (fermented soybean paste stew, page 72). Also, most Korean households use a measuring trick for determining the right rice-to-water ratio. Simply put your index finger on the surface of the rice and make sure the water comes up to your first knuckle.

해물파전 **HAEMUL PAJEON**

SAVORY SEAFOOD PANCAKES

Serves 4 / Prep time: 15 minutes / **Cook time:** 10 minutes

Literally translated, pajeon means green onions (pa) and flour batter (jeon). This version is a savory, fluffy pancake with crispy edges dotted with a variety of seafood—nothing like sweet pancakes smothered in maple syrup. You can buy a frozen seafood medley that has many seafood options already cleaned for you, or you can buy the seafood fresh and prepare it yourself.

For the dipping sauce

2 tablespoons soy sauce

2 tablespoons
  rice vinegar

For the pajeon

¾ cup all-purpose flour

2 tablespoons
  potato starch

2 teaspoons kosher salt

1½ cups club soda

4 tablespoons vegetable
  oil, divided

4 green onions,
  roots cut off

1 cup seafood (like
  shrimp, squid, and
  clams), cleaned and
  coarsely chopped into
  ½ inch pieces

1 Fresno chile,
  thinly sliced

1. **To make the dipping sauce:** In a small bowl, combine the soy sauce and vinegar, and set aside.

2. **To make the pajeon:** In a large bowl, whisk together the flour, potato starch, salt, and club soda. The batter should be fluffy and thin.

3. In a medium nonstick pan, heat 2 tablespoons of the vegetable oil over medium-high heat.

4. Dip the green onions in the batter, then arrange all of them in the heated pan at the same time. Cook for 2 minutes.

5. Combine the seafood and chile with the remaining batter and add it to the pan, making sure to fill the whole pan with the seafood and tucking it between and on top of the green onions. Cook for 2 minutes more, then flip the pancake and add the remaining 2 tablespoons of oil around the sides. Continue cooking until both sides of the pancake are golden brown and cooked through.

6. Place the haemul pajeon on a large platter. Using kitchen scissors, cut the pancake into 2-inch pieces. Serve right away with the dipping sauce.

대구전 DAEGUJEON
BREADED COD FILLETS

Serves 4 / Prep time: 15 minutes / **Cook time:** 10 minutes

There is a variety of jeon (flour batter) savory pancakes that can fill the Korean table, but this recipe focuses on fish. You can use this same method and batter with many ingredients, like shrimp, zucchini, or sweet potatoes, to make different varieties. Cod is the most common fish jeon because of its neutral, meaty flavor.

For the dipping sauce

2 tablespoons soy sauce
2 tablespoons
  rice vinegar

For the daegujeon

1 pound cod fillets
2 teaspoons kosher salt
1 teaspoon garlic powder
1 cup all-purpose flour
2 eggs
2 tablespoons
  vegetable oil

1. **To make the dipping sauce:** In a small bowl, combine the soy sauce and vinegar, and set aside.

2. **To make the daegujeon:** Pat the cod dry with paper towels. Cut the fish into 2-inch pieces. Season both sides of the pieces with the salt and garlic powder.

3. In one shallow bowl, place the flour. In a second shallow bowl, beat the eggs. Dip each piece of cod first into the flour, then into the eggs.

4. In a medium nonstick pan, heat the vegetable oil over medium-high heat. Cook the breaded cod pieces for about 4 minutes per side, or until golden brown. Then let them sit on a paper towel to remove excess oil.

5. Place all of the daegujeon on a serving platter and serve either warm or at room temperature with the dipping sauce.

계란말이 **GYERAN MARI**
ROLLED EGG OMELET

Makes 1 roll / Prep time: 10 minutes / **Cook time:** 10 minutes

Unlike the simple Gyeranjjim (steamed eggs, page 54) from chapter 3, these rolled omelets will give you the chance to add some delicious fillings. There's a little bit of technique you'll need to warm up to, but you will quickly get into a rhythm of pouring the egg mixture into the hot pan and making these fluffy, tasty rolls. This recipe uses bell peppers and green onions, but feel free to try other fillings, like dry roasted seaweed or a bit of mozzarella cheese.

5 large eggs

½ red bell pepper, finely chopped

2 green onions, finely chopped

2 teaspoons garlic powder

2 teaspoons kosher salt

3 tablespoons vegetable oil, divided

1. In a medium bowl, beat the eggs. Add the bell pepper, green onions, garlic powder, and salt.

2. In a medium nonstick pan, heat 1 teaspoon of vegetable oil over medium-low heat. Pour ⅓ of the egg mixture in the pan, tilting the pan to ensure the egg mixture covers the bottom.

3. Cook for about 3 minutes, until the top of the egg starts to set. Using chopsticks or a spatula, start from one end and roll the omelet away from you until you get to the end. While the omelet is still in the pan, add another 1 teaspoon of vegetable oil and another ⅓ of the egg mixture to the side of the pan that is closest to you. Swirl the pan so the egg mixture connects to the first roll, wait until it sets, then roll again starting with the rolled end. Repeat one more time with the remaining 1 teaspoon of oil and the remaining ⅓ of the egg mixture.

4. Gently transfer the omelet to a cutting board and slice it into 1-inch-thick pieces. Arrange the slices on a large serving platter.

PREP TIP: Be careful not to heat the pan too high or the eggs will become rubbery.

만두 MANDU
PORK AND KIMCHI DUMPLINGS

Makes 20 dumplings / Prep time: 30 minutes, plus 30 minutes to chill /
Cook time: 15 minutes

These tasty little dumplings can be filled with just about anything, but my favorite is pork and kimchi. This combination is a simple but powerful duo that brings ultimate flavor in a little package. They're a true treat because they take some time to make. To save yourself some labor, I recommend using mandu wrappers (which are the same as gyoza or wonton wrappers).

For the dipping sauce

2 tablespoons soy sauce
2 tablespoons
   rice vinegar

For the mandu

8 ounces ground pork
½ cup Baechu Kimchi
   (napa cabbage
   kimchi, page 42)
   or store-bought
   kimchi, drained and
   finely chopped
1 green onion,
   finely chopped
1 large egg, beaten
1 teaspoon garlic powder
1 teaspoon potato starch
½ teaspoon kosher salt
20 round (about ½
   [12-ounce] package)
   mandu dumpling
   wrappers
2 tablespoons
   vegetable oil

1. **To make the dipping sauce:** In a small bowl, combine the soy sauce and vinegar, and set aside.

2. **To make the mandu:** In a medium bowl, use your hands to mix together the pork, kimchi, green onion, egg, garlic powder, potato starch, and salt. Cover and refrigerate the bowl for 30 minutes, so the filling is easier to handle.

3. Pour some water into a small bowl to use to help seal the mandu. Lay one of the mandu wrappers on a work surface. Add 1 teaspoon of chilled filling to the center of a mandu wrapper.

4. Using your fingers, wet half of the wrapper's edge with water. Seal the wrapper to make a half-moon, pushing excess air out, then quickly bring the two points together and press firmly to seal. Gently flatten the bottoms so the mandu sits upright. Set the dumpling on a large platter or baking sheet. Repeat with the other wrappers and the rest of the filling.

5. In a medium nonstick pan, heat the vegetable oil over medium-heat. Working in batches as necessary, add a single layer of dumplings and fry for about 2 minutes, until the bottoms are golden brown. Carefully add about 2 tablespoons of water (you will hear a loud hiss as the water hits the pan), then immediately reduce the heat to low, cover the pan with a lid, and cook for 5 to 8 minutes, until the water has evaporated and the dumplings are shiny.

6. Serve right away on a large serving platter with the dipping sauce.

MAKE-AHEAD TIP: If you prepare the mandu ahead of time, refrigerate them in a covered container, and then cook within 24 hours. You can also freeze prepared mandu separated from each other on a parchment-covered baking sheet. Once frozen, store them in a freezer container. Use the frozen dumplings within three months.

KOREAN CORN CHEESE

Serves 4 / Prep time: 15 minutes / **Cook time:** 15 minutes

Korean corn cheese was originally made as an anju dish (food made to eat while you're drinking alcoholic beverages). Because of its popularity, it's become a must-have item on KBBQ menus across the United States. The melted cheese on top of buttery corn goes so well with all of the brighter and fermented flavors on the Korean barbecue table. Fresh or canned corn works.

2 tablespoons
unsalted butter

2 (15-ounce) cans corn,
drained, or 1½ cups
fresh corn

½ small yellow onion,
finely chopped

½ red bell pepper,
finely chopped

1 tablespoon
minced garlic

3 tablespoons
mayonnaise

1 teaspoon white sugar

½ teaspoon kosher salt

1 cup shredded
mozzarella cheese

1. Set the broiler to high.

2. In a medium oven-safe pan over medium-high heat, melt the butter slightly for about 1 minute. Once it's melted, add the corn, onion, bell pepper, and garlic. Sauté for 5 minutes, stirring to help the moisture evaporate.

3. Turn off the heat and add the mayonnaise, sugar, and salt and stir until evenly incorporated. Top the corn mixture with the mozzarella.

4. Put the pan under the broiler for about 5 minutes, until the cheese melts and slightly browns.

PREP TIP: If you have different compartments built around your grill pan, you can add the corn mixture and top it with cheese directly on your grill. When the cheese is melted, it's ready to eat.

김치찌개 KIMCHI JJIGAE
KIMCHI STEW

Serves 4 / Prep time: 30 minutes / **Cook time:** 45 minutes

The layers of flavor in this sumptuous stew come from the kimchi and pork belly, but you can substitute the pork with seafood or beef or keep it plant-based with plenty of earthy, dried shiitake mushrooms. The kimchi should be well fermented (sometimes it's called sour, at least a month old) in order to get the best, deepest flavor in the stew.

1 pound (½-inch thick) skinless pork belly, cut into ½-inch strips

1 small yellow onion, thinly sliced

1 teaspoon kosher salt

2 cups Baechu Kimchi (napa cabbage kimchi, page 42) or other well-fermented kimchi, coarsely chopped, juice strained and reserved

4 cups water

2 tablespoons fish sauce

2 tablespoons minced garlic

1 tablespoon coarse gochugaru flakes

1 tablespoon toasted sesame oil

1 (14-ounce) package firm tofu, drained and cut into ½-inch cubes

2 green onions, finely chopped, for garnish

1 teaspoon sesame seeds, for garnish

1. In a medium pot, heat the pork over medium-high heat for about 5 minutes per side, until the meat crisps up and the fat renders. Add the onions and salt and cook for about 5 minutes, stirring, until the onions have softened. Add the kimchi (reserving the juice) and sauté for 5 minutes more.

2. To the same pot, add the water, fish sauce, reserved kimchi juice, garlic, gochugaru, and oil. Stir everything together, bring the mixture to a boil, then reduce the heat to medium so the mixture reaches a gentle boil. Cook for about 20 minutes.

3. Add the tofu cubes to the top of the stew and continue to gently boil for 5 minutes.

4. Garnish the stew with green onions and sesame seeds and serve right away.

MAKE-AHEAD TIP: This stew can be made days before. Simply let the stew cool, then store it in a covered container in the refrigerator. Bring it back up to a full boil for 5 minutes before serving.

물냉면 **MUL NAENGMYEON**
COLD NOODLE SOUP

Serves 4 / Prep time: 1 hour, plus 3 hours to freeze / **Cook time:** 1 hour 15 minutes

After all of the heat, spice, flavors, and textures of Korean barbecue, it's nice, and traditional, to finish the meal with a refreshing bowl of cold noodle soup. This recipe can also be enjoyed on its own as a single serving for one person. When you buy the brisket, ask the butcher to slice a whole piece off for you so you can slice it at the end, unless you can find it already packaged in this small amount.

For the broth

8 ounces brisket

1 large yellow
  onion, halved

5 garlic cloves, halved

1 (½-inch) knob ginger,
  peeled and halved

1 teaspoon white sugar

2 tablespoons soup
  soy sauce (or regular
  soy sauce)

12 cups water

Kosher salt

For the pickled radish

1 cup (about ½ pound)
  mu (Korean radish), cut
  into 2-inch strips

2 tablespoons
  rice vinegar

1 tablespoon kosher salt

2 tablespoons
  white sugar

For serving

1 (12-ounce)
  package dried
  naengmyeon noodles

2 Persian cucumbers,
  julienned

1 small Asian pear,
  thinly sliced

2 hard-boiled eggs,
  peeled and halved

1 teaspoon sesame seeds

Korean hot mustard,
  for serving

Rice vinegar, for serving

1. **To make the broth:** In a large pot over high heat, combine the brisket, onion, garlic, ginger, sugar, soup soy sauce, and water. Bring the mixture to a boil, then reduce the heat to low and simmer for 1 hour, skimming the foam off, until the brisket is tender. You'll continue making the broth in step 4.

2. **To make the pickled radish:** While the broth is simmering, in a small bowl, combine the radish, vinegar, salt, and sugar. Set aside until the broth is done and juice has been extracted from the radish.

3. Remove the brisket from the large pot, cut it into thin ⅛-inch slices, and set aside.

4. Using a strainer, strain the broth into a large bowl. Add the juice from the pickled radish, setting aside the pickled radishes themselves. Working 1 teaspoon at a time, add salt in increments to the broth to taste.

5. Transfer the broth to a covered container and put it in the freezer for about 3 hours, until its consistency turns slushy. If it's frozen solid, let it thaw until it gets back to the slushy consistency.

6. **To serve:** Cook the noodles according to the package instructions. Drain and immediately rinse them with cold water until the noodles are chilled. Divide the noodles evenly into four serving bowls.

7. Layer the cucumbers, pears, pickled radish, and half an egg on top of each bowl. Sprinkle each serving with sesame seeds. Pour about 2½ cups of slushy broth around the noodles in each bowl. Serve with Korean hot mustard and rice vinegar on the side.

MAKE-AHEAD TIP: The broth and toppings can be made ahead of time, but the noodles will need to be cooked and eaten right away.

PREP TIP: Soup soy sauce (see Ganjang 간장 Soy Sauce, page 12) is the best ingredient to use in this recipe, but all-purpose soy sauce is okay to use as an alternative. It will change the broth's color and taste slightly saltier.

된장찌개 DOENJANG JJIGAE

FERMENTED SOYBEAN PASTE STEW

Serves 4 / Prep time: 30 minutes / **Cook time:** 40 minutes

Doenjang jjigae tastes very complex because of the fermented soybean paste used in the recipe. When you rinse your rice before cooking it (see Bap, step 1, page 62), save the water from the last two times you rinse the grains. The water should look cloudy from the starch released by the rice, and that can become the main binder that holds this stew together.

8 ounces pork butt, cut into ½-inch strips

1 small zucchini, halved and thinly sliced

5 dried shiitake mushrooms, broken into small pieces

1 small yellow onion, halved and thinly sliced

1 teaspoon kosher salt

4 cups rice water (or regular tap water)

3 tablespoons doenjang

2 tablespoons minced garlic

1 teaspoon coarse gochugaru flakes

1 (14-ounce) package firm tofu, drained and cut into ½-inch cubes

2 green onions, finely chopped, for garnish

1 Fresno chile, finely chopped, for garnish

1 tablespoon toasted sesame oil

1. In a medium pot over medium-high heat, brown the pork butt for about 5 minutes per side. Add the zucchini, mushrooms, onion, and salt and sauté for about 5 minutes.

2. Add the rice water, doenjang, garlic, and gochugaru and stir everything together. Bring the stew to a boil, then reduce the heat to medium and maintain a medium boil for about 20 minutes.

3. Add the tofu cubes to the top of the stew and continue to boil for 5 minutes.

4. Garnish the stew with the green onions and chile and drizzle it with oil. Serve right in the pot (use a trivet).

MAKE-AHEAD TIP: This stew can be made days before. Simply let the stew cool, then store it in a covered container in the refrigerator. Bring back up to a boil for 5 minutes before serving.

PREP TIP: If you don't want the soybean texture from the doenjang in the stew, you can push the paste through a sieve when the stew is boiling.

비빔국수 **BIBIM GUKSU**
MIXED NOODLES

Serves 4 / Prep time: 30 minutes / **Cook time:** 5 minutes

Bibim guksu is a noodle dish in a wonderfully dressed spicy sauce. This recipe calls for dried somyeon noodles, which are made with wheat flour, cooked for only a short time, and cooled immediately for a great chewy texture. Feel free to add any veggies you like.

½ cup Baechu Kimchi (napa cabbage kimchi, page 42) or store-bought kimchi, strained, liquid reserved, and finely chopped

4 tablespoons gochujang

3 tablespoons rice vinegar

2 tablespoons plum syrup

1 teaspoon white sugar

1 tablespoon soy sauce

1 tablespoon toasted sesame oil

1 tablespoon minced garlic

1 (12-ounce) package dried somyeon noodles

2 Persian cucumbers, julienned

2 cups julienned purple cabbage

2 hard-boiled eggs, peeled and halved

1. Check how much liquid was strained from the kimchi; you should have ½ cup. In a large bowl, combine the gochujang, vinegar, plum syrup, sugar, soy sauce, oil, kimchi juice, kimchi, and garlic. Mix them together, and set aside.

2. Cook the noodles according to the package instructions. Drain and immediately rinse them with cold water until the noodles are chilled. Add the cooked noodles to the large bowl with the sauce and toss until evenly incorporated.

3. Divide the noodles evenly into four serving bowls. Top the noodles with the cucumber, cabbage, and egg.

볶음밥 BOKKEUMBAP

FRIED RICE

Serves 4 / Prep time: 15 minutes **/ Cook time:** 25 minutes

You know those leftover bits and caramelized drippings that build up on the grill pan? Here's a delicious way to use them. All you need is day-old chilled rice, a few drops of soy sauce, toasted sesame oil, and a few other taste enhancers, and you'll enjoy "cleaning up" your grill!

4 cups Bap (steamed short-grain rice, page 62), refrigerated

2 tablespoons vegetable oil (optional)

1 small yellow onion, thinly sliced

1 cup Baechu Kimchi (napa cabbage kimchi, page 42) or other well-fermented kimchi, chopped

2 tablespoons minced garlic

2 tablespoons soy sauce

2 tablespoons toasted sesame oil

1 tablespoon coarse gochugaru flakes

2 green onions, finely chopped, for garnish

1. In a large bowl, break apart any large clumps of the refrigerated leftover rice, and set aside.

2. Heat a grill pan over medium-high heat. If the grill pan doesn't have enough fat (at least 2 tablespoons) from the drippings, pour in the vegetable oil. Add the onion and cook for about 10 minutes, until lightly browned and softened. Add the kimchi and cook for about 5 minutes, stirring occasionally.

3. Reduce the heat to medium. In the same grill pan, add the rice, garlic, soy sauce, sesame oil, and gochugaru and cook for about 5 minutes, stirring, until most of the moisture has evaporated and the rice is heated through.

4. Flatten the rice over the bottom of the grill pan and let it brown for about 3 minutes, until the bottom is crisp. Turn off the heat and top the rice with the green onions.

5. Serve the bokkeumbap right off the grill pan, or scoop it into individual bowls.

PREP TIP: This recipe is made for the grill pan because it will use all the drippings. But you can also chop up leftover proteins and sauté the rice with the kimchi, garlic, and onions in a pan on the stove.

SUBAK HWACHAE, WATERMELON PUNCH; PAGE 79

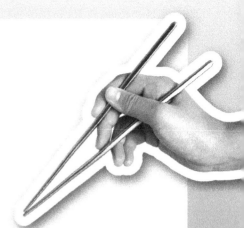

DRINKS *AND* DESSERTS

보리차 **BORICHA**

BARLEY TEA

Makes 4 cups / Cook time: 12 minutes

Boricha is a Korean tea with a lovely nutty flavor. Part of the popularity of the drink is that it's full of antioxidants. You can find the roasted barley kernels portioned out into individual tea bags or packaged in large bags as loose kernels. This recipe yields four servings, but you can make a huge batch and store it in the refrigerator for five days. Serve the tea piping hot or chilled throughout your KBBQ.

4 cups hot water

¼ cup roasted barley kernels

1. Pour the water into a kettle or pot and bring it to a boil.

2. Add the roasted barley kernels and boil for 10 minutes.

3. Strain and serve the boricha right away, or let it cool to room temperature, then refrigerate it to serve cold.

수박화채 SUBAK HWACHAE
WATERMELON PUNCH

Serves 8 / Prep time: 20 minutes

Traditionally a refreshing drink for Korea's hot summer days, this watermelon punch proves perfect all year round to mellow out all of the heat and spices of KBBQ. Dress it up with other fruit, like grapes and blueberries, or serve it with flair by hollowing out a small watermelon to use as a punch bowl. If you'd like an extra fun kick, add some soju to the punch.

9 cups cubed watermelon (from about 2 large watermelons)

2 cups balled watermelon (from about ½ small watermelon)

1 cup balled cantaloupe (from about ½ large cantaloupe)

1 cup quartered strawberries

4 cups ginger ale

Ice cubes, for chilling and serving

1. In a blender, blend the watermelon cubes to make about 2 cups of watermelon juice.

2. In a punch bowl or pitcher combine the watermelon balls, cantaloupe balls, and strawberries. Add the ginger ale, then the watermelon juice. Fill the bowl or pitcher with ice cubes and serve immediately.

수정과 SUJEONGGWA

KOREAN CINNAMON PUNCH

Serves 4 / Prep time: 10 minutes, plus 9 hours to chill / **Cook time:** 1 hour

This traditional sweet cinnamon punch, so reminiscent of autumn, can be served while you're enjoying Korean barbecue, or afterward as a dessert. In fact, it is said to aid digestion, which may be a good thing after indulging in KBBQ! Its sweetness is balanced by the pine nuts and it should be sipped at a slow and leisurely pace.

5 cinnamon sticks

½ cup peeled and
   coarsely sliced
   fresh ginger

8 cups water

1 cup lightly packed dark
   brown sugar

2 dried whole
   persimmons, quartered

12 or 20 pine nuts,
   for serving

Ice, for serving

1. In a medium pot over high heat, combine the cinnamon, ginger, and water and bring to a boil. Cover the pot, reduce the heat to medium-low, and simmer for 45 minutes.

2. Add the sugar and continue to simmer for 15 minutes more, stirring to make sure the sugar dissolves.

3. Remove the pot from the heat. Discard the cinnamon sticks and ginger and add the dried persimmons.

4. Let the punch cool to room temperature for about 1 hour. Then, pour it into a pitcher with a lid and chill it in the refrigerator for 9 hours or overnight.

5. When you're ready to serve, place 3 to 5 pine nuts and the ice in each of four glasses before pouring the punch.

GINGER-TANGERINE GRANITA

Serves 4 / Prep time: 15 minutes, plus 4 hours to freeze

Ginger and tangerines are great palate cleansers after a full-flavored meal, and this combination is also a nice little nod to Jeju Island, the largest island off of South Korea, known for its beaches, volcanoes, and, most importantly here, its citrus fruit. Time is the main ingredient for this recipe; it needs little hands-on tending. If you can't find tangerines, oranges will do.

3 cups peeled tangerine slices (from about 12 tangerines)

¼ cup freshly squeezed lemon juice

1 tablespoon peeled grated fresh ginger

3 tablespoons white sugar

½ teaspoon kosher salt

½ cup water

1. In a blender, blend the tangerines until mostly smooth. Add the lemon juice, ginger, sugar, salt, and water and pulse until the mixture has the consistency of a smoothie.

2. Pour the mixture into a shallow baking dish and freeze it for 1 hour, then fluff the mixture with a fork. Freeze and fluff the mixture 3 more times, until all of the liquid has turned into uniform ice crystals. After that, keep it in the freezer until ready to serve.

3. Scoop the ginger-tangerine granita into individual small bowls and serve.

MAKE-AHEAD TIP: The ginger-tangerine granita can be made ahead of time and kept in a covered container in the freezer for one week before it starts forming harder ice crystals. Make sure to fluff it with a fork before serving.

ROASTED PERSIMMONS WITH YOGURT, HONEY, AND CINNAMON

Serves 4 / Prep time: 35 minutes / **Cook time:** 20 minutes

Persimmons are a popular fruit in Korea. After all, South Korea (along with China and Japan) is one of the top producers of the fruit. They can be eaten fresh or cooked, and they have a nutty sweet taste that is simply delicious. When roasted, a whole new set of warm, comforting flavors come out on display. Plain Greek yogurt balances the sweetness of the honey, and the cinnamon sprinkles add warmth.

2 Fuyu persimmons

1 tablespoon vegetable oil

2 cups plain Greek yogurt

4 tablespoons honey

2 teaspoons ground cinnamon

Flaky sea salt, for serving

1. Preheat the oven to 375°F. Line a baking sheet with parchment or foil.

2. Cut the top and bottom off of the persimmons and use a vegetable peeler to remove the skin. Slice across the persimmons to make ¼-inch circles and coat them with the vegetable oil.

3. Place the persimmon rounds on the prepared baking sheet and roast for 20 minutes, until soft and slightly golden. Let the persimmon rounds cool for about 30 minutes, until they reach room temperature.

4. To serve, divide the persimmons equally into four bowls and add ¼ cup of plain Greek yogurt to each. Drizzle each serving with 1 tablespoon of honey. Sprinkle each with ½ teaspoon of the cinnamon and the flaky sea salt to taste.

NO-CHURN KOREAN INSTANT COFFEE ICE CREAM

Makes 6 cups / Prep time: 10 minutes, plus 6 hours to freeze

This no-churn ice cream is an homage to the popularity of Korean instant coffee. In Korea, many people start their day with a quick caffeine beverage that has the sweetness already added (instead of waiting for a cup of coffee to brew, and then adding sugar). The little instant coffee packages include various styles of coffee and can go head-to-head with any barista's brew. The Korean instant coffee mix called for in this recipe works well because it has a lighter coffee flavor than most other instant coffee crystals. If you can't find it, a lighter roast of any instant coffee will work.

1 (14-ounce) can sweetened condensed milk

2 tablespoons Korean instant coffee

1 teaspoon kosher salt

2 cups heavy (whipping) cream

1. In a medium bowl, mix together the condensed milk, Korean instant coffee, and salt.

2. In a separate larger bowl, use a hand mixer to whisk the cream for 3 to 5 minutes, until stiff peaks form.

3. Gently fold the condensed milk mixture into the whipped cream.

4. Pour the mixture into a 9-by-5-inch loaf pan, cover it with plastic wrap, and place it in the refrigerator for 6 hours, or until hardened.

5. Scoop out the ice cream when you're ready to serve.

KOREAN BARBECUE MENUS

The combinations you have to play with are infinite, so it can be difficult to settle on a menu for your Korean barbecue. For this reason, I offer six menus for you as a guide. They include components from each chapter and take into account flavors, textures, food combinations, timing, and ingredients. For all of the menus, I have made sure to include some make-ahead dishes so you won't have to prepare everything the day of. There's even a vegetarian menu. Some of the menus serve four; others serve six or eight. If necessary, ask your friends and family to make a dish or two to help you out.

KBBQ MENU #1 for 4 People

MAIN
Dwaeji Bulgogi, Spicy Marinated Pork (page 27)

BANCHANS
Sangchu, Red Leaf Lettuce (page 7)

Ssamjang, Fermented Soybean and Chili Dipping Sauce (page 36)

Pa Muchim, Green Onion Salad (page 48)

Oi Muchim, Spicy Cucumber Salad (page 47)

SMALL PLATE
Bap, Steamed Short-Grain Rice (page 62)

DESSERT OR BEVERAGE
Boricha, Barley Tea (page 78)

KBBQ MENU #2 for 4 People

MAIN
Bulgogi, Thinly Sliced Marinated Beef (page 22)

BANCHANS
Baechu Kimchi, Napa Cabbage Kimchi (page 42)

Jangajji, Pickled Onions and Chiles (page 51)

Kongnamul Muchim, Seasoned Soybean Sprouts (page 58)

SMALL PLATE
Bap, Steamed Short-Grain Rice (page 62)

DESSERT OR BEVERAGE
Roasted Persimmons with Yogurt, Honey, and Cinnamon (page 82)

KBBQ MENU #3 for 6 People

MAINS

Dak Galbi, Spicy Marinated Chicken (page 26)

Deungsim, Marinated Strip Steak (page 24)

Samgyeopsal, Pork Belly (page 39)

BANCHANS

Sangchu, Red Leaf Lettuce (page 7)

Kkaennip, Perilla Leaves (page 7)

Gireumjang, Salt and Sesame Oil Dipping Sauce (page 6)

Ssamjang, Fermented Soybean and Chili Dipping Sauce (page 36)

Baechu Geotjeori, Fresh Kimchi (page 44)

SMALL PLATES

Daegujeon, Breaded Cod Fillets (page 64)

Gyeran Mari, Rolled Egg Omelet (page 65)

DESSERT OR BEVERAGE

Sujeonggwa, Korean Cinnamon Punch (page 80)

VEGETARIAN KBBQ MENU #4 for 6 People

MAINS

Oyster Mushroom Bulgogi (page 35)

Gochujang Eggplant Gui (page 34)

Jackfruit Bulgogi (page 33)

BANCHANS

Ssam Mu, Marinated Radish Wraps (page 50)

Sangchu, Red Leaf Lettuce (page 7)

Pa Muchim, Green Onion Salad (page 48)

Gamja Jorim, Sweet Braised Potatoes (page 52)

Dubu Jorim, Spicy Braised Tofu (page 55)

Roasted Broccoli with Sweetened Gochujang Sauce (page 56)

SMALL PLATE

Bap, Steamed Short-Grain Rice (page 62)

DESSERTS OR BEVERAGES

Subak Hwachae, Watermelon Punch (page 79)

Ginger-Tangerine Granita (page 81)

KBBQ MENU #5 for 8 People

MAINS
Galbi, Marinated Short Ribs
(page 23)

Maekjeok, Doenjang Marinated Pork (page 28)

Dwaeji Bulgogi, Spicy Marinated Pork (page 27)

BANCHANS
Green Onion and Vinegar
Sauce (page 38)

Baechu Kimchi, Napa Cabbage
Kimchi (page 42)

Kkakdugi, Radish Kimchi
(page 46)

Sangchu Geotjeori, Korean Lettuce Salad (page 49)

Ssam Mu, Marinated Radish
Wraps (page 50)

Eomuk Bokkeum, Stir-Fried Fish
Cake (page 59)

SMALL PLATES
Bap, Steamed Short-Grain Rice
(page 62)

Haemul Pajeon, Savory Seafood Pancakes (page 63)

Doenjang Jjigae, Fermented
Soybean Paste Stew (page 72)

DESSERT OR BEVERAGE
No-Churn Korean Instant
Coffee Ice Cream (page 83)

KBBQ MENU #6 for 8 People

MAINS
Ojingeo Gui, Spicy Marinated
Squid (page 31)

Saeu Gui, Marinated Shrimp
(page 30)

Dak Bulgogi, Marinated
Chicken (page 25)

Chadol Bagi, Beef Brisket
(page 39)

BANCHANS
Baechu Kimchi, Napa Cabbage
Kimchi (page 42)

Gamja Salad, Korean Potato
Salad (page 53)

Roasted Broccoli with Sweetened Gochujang Sauce
(page 56)

SMALL PLATES
Kimchi Jjigae, Kimchi Stew
(page 69)

Korean Corn Cheese (page 68)

Bibim Guksu, Mixed Noodles
(page 73)

DESSERT AND BEVERAGE
Roasted Persimmons with
Yogurt, Honey, and Cinnamon
(page 82)

Subak Hwachae, Watermelon
Punch (page 79)

GOCHUJANG EGGPLANT GUI, PAGE 34

MEASUREMENT CONVERSIONS

VOLUME EQUIVALENTS	U.S. STANDARD	U.S. STANDARD (OUNCES)	METRIC (APPROXIMATE)
LIQUID	2 tablespoons	1 fl. oz.	30 mL
	¼ cup	2 fl. oz.	60 mL
	½ cup	4 fl. oz.	120 mL
	1 cup	8 fl. oz.	240 mL
	1½ cups	12 fl. oz.	355 mL
	2 cups or 1 pint	16 fl. oz.	475 mL
	4 cups or 1 quart	32 fl. oz.	1 L
	1 gallon	128 fl. oz.	4 L
DRY	⅛ teaspoon	—	0.5 mL
	¼ teaspoon	—	1 mL
	½ teaspoon	—	2 mL
	¾ teaspoon	—	4 mL
	1 teaspoon	—	5 mL
	1 tablespoon	—	15 mL
	¼ cup	—	59 mL
	⅓ cup	—	79 mL
	½ cup	—	118 mL
	⅔ cup	—	156 mL
	¾ cup	—	177 mL
	1 cup	—	235 mL
	2 cups or 1 pint	—	475 mL
	3 cups	—	700 mL
	4 cups or 1 quart	—	1 L
	½ gallon	—	2 L
	1 gallon	—	4 L

OVEN TEMPERATURES

FAHRENHEIT	CELSIUS (APPROXIMATE)
250°F	120°C
300°F	150°C
325°F	165°C
350°F	180°C
375°F	190°C
400°F	200°C
425°F	220°C
450°F	230°C

WEIGHT EQUIVALENTS

U.S. STANDARD	METRIC (APPROXIMATE)
½ ounce	15 g
1 ounce	30 g
2 ounces	60 g
4 ounces	115 g
8 ounces	225 g
12 ounces	340 g
16 ounces or 1 pound	455 g

RESOURCES

If you don't have a Korean grocery store nearby, you can definitely order ingredients online. The price of shipping will make the ingredients a bit more expensive, but it might save you from hunting around at lots of grocery stores. Some of these stores are limited by location for shipping, but the bigger chains, like H Mart, will be able to reach more people.

- HMart.com

- ArirangUSA.net

- KoaMarket.com

- KimcMarket.com

- SeoulMills.com

- Gochujar.com

- SFMart.com

- sayweee.com

- HanyangMart.com

- amazon.com/Korean-Grocery/s?k=Korean+Grocery

INDEX

ACKNOWLEDGMENTS

I can't imagine even attempting to write this cookbook without the guidance of my senior editor, Cecily McAndrews. I'm so thankful for her help in making sure that this book had an authentic voice to it and for answering all of the many, many questions I had. She has made this whole process a delight!

The detailed eye provided by my developmental editor, Caryn Abramowitz, was so impressively impeccable. I feel very lucky to have had the honor of working with her. I thank her for making sure this cookbook is polished and has the shine that it deserves.

A big thank you to my acquisitions editor, Ashley Popp, for initially finding me and bringing me onto this project in such a welcoming way.

And last but not least, I'd like to give my deepest gratitude and appreciation to my husband, Todd Lind. I'm so thankful that I have a partner that gives me the huge amount of support that he does. He has lovingly helped me get through the months of writing and recipe testing and rewriting to make this cookbook happen. He is my rock. Love you, babe, so very much.

ABOUT THE AUTHOR

Sara Upshaw is the creator of *Kimchi Halfie*, a blog that showcases the foods she grew up eating with the versions she's created over the years in her own kitchen. Her Korean roots and the Pacific Northwest, where she's lived most of her life, have had the deepest influences on her recipes. Her photos, videos, and stories celebrate her love of feeding people near and far, strangers and loved ones. She truly enjoys teaching others the skills involved in home cooking. And her wish for everyone who savors her dishes and recipes is that they taste full-bodied flavors and comfort in every single bite.

CPSIA information can be obtained
at www.ICGtesting.com
Printed in the USA
JSHW032114041021
19277JS00002B/6